人生でひとつでも、夢中になれることを見つけられた人間は幸せ者だ。
ある日、雪とスキーに魅せられた男が、新たな雪と感動を求めて旅に出た。
スキーを担ぎ、国境のない地図を片手に。

JN125198

プロローグ

まるでSF映画の世界に迷い込んだような気分だった。
ゴーストタウンと化した都市。
一様にマスクを着用し、沈黙している人々。
当たり前と思っていたことが、全て塗り替えられていく。
約束された安全や将来などないことは知っていながら、何の根拠もなく「大丈夫だろう」と高を括っていた。
まさか、こんな時代に人類史上稀に見る災難が地球規模で降りかかるだなんて…。

2020年4月某日、札幌市の自宅。居間にヨガマットを広げ、ひたすら腕立て伏せに励んでいた。何に向かっているのかは自分でもわからない。ただ、こうでもしていないと頭がおかしくなりそうだった。世の中が「ステイホーム」という合言葉のもと、外出を極限に抑える状況にあったからだ。
さてさて…。本編に入る前に、俺の自己紹介を簡単にしておこう。
児玉毅、47歳。職業スキーヤー、趣味スキー。大学時代にスキーにハマりすぎ、卒業後も2年限定と決めて全精力をスキーに捧げてみた結果、満足するどころかスキーの限りない魅力に気付いてしまい、スキーだけで生きていく決心をして自称「プロスキーヤー」に。若い頃は

崖を滑るスキーや前人未到の斜面を滑る遠征で世界中を駆けずり回って過ごしたが、運良く生き残ったお陰で人並みに幸せな結婚をして子供にも恵まれた。それでもなお世界中の雪山を一生かけて滑りまくる野心は潰えることなく、2012年から「地球を滑る旅」を佐藤圭くん（49歳、職業カメラマン、趣味カメラ）とスタート。書籍を出版するという文化的行為により「ただ滑りたい」という欲求をカモフラージュをすることに成功し、家族の理解もゲット。このまま足腰が立つ90歳くらいまでは、順調に世界中を滑り歩く予定…の男である。
ただ滑っているだけでも超ハッピーなのに、スキーに没頭している姿を発信し、スキーファンと感動を共にすることで心から喜んでもらえるのだから、こんな幸せな人生はない。旅やスキーをする上で各国の政情や地球温暖化をはじめとする環境問題など懸念材料はあるけれど、スキーを続けていくかどうかは自分のやる気次第だと思っていた。そう、コロナ禍によって価値観がひっくり返るまでは…。まず、予定していたスキーの仕事が全てキャンセルとなり、スキー産業自体が自粛状態に。それでも「密を避けられるスキーは健康維持に最高でしょう！」と山に行っていたら、「もし山で怪我などされたら大迷惑！ 医療崩壊寸前なのに！」という具合に、山に入ることさえも社会悪とみなされるようになった。こうして、自分からスキーを取って

しまったら、就職した経験もないただのプータローだという現実に、47歳にして初めて気付かされたのだ。「やばくない？」今まで信じてきたことが大きく揺れ動いていた。

「しばらく地球を滑る旅は難しそうだね…」圭くんと電話で話していた。レバノンに始まり、モロッコ、アイスランド、カシミール、ロシア、ギリシャ、中国と順調に旅を重ねてきた俺たちだったが、コロナの世界的な流行によって8回目の旅は中止を余儀なくされた。俺のパソコンには「地球を滑る旅　候補地」というファイルがあって、それを開くと様々な国を滑るための情報が集積されている。行きたい場所が多すぎて、1年に1箇所ペースでは生きている間に全て行き尽くせない計算になる。だからこそ1年1年が大事だと思っていた。しかし、逆立ちをしたって行けない現実は変わらないのだから、この状況を少しでもプラスに捉えなければ。そうだ。スキー好きが高じてプロスキーヤーになった俺だけど、ここ数年はスケジュールに追われることが多く、自分の滑りに没頭する時間は少なくなっていた。今、真っ白なスケジュールを眺めながら、来る日も来る日も何の疑いもなく滑り続けていた20代前半の時を思い出していた。テレビを消し、携帯電話から離れ、ゆっくりと本を開く時間ができた。腕立て、腹筋、懸垂、

Prolog

I felt like I'd gotten lost in the world of a science fiction movie.
Our city was like a ghost town.
Everyone was wearing a mask and was staying silent.
Everything that I'd taken for granted had become a thing of the past. I knew that there was no such thing as a promise of security or the future, but without any reason, I was thinking, "We will be okay." I could not believe that we were facing a global-scale pandemic, something hardly ever experienced in human history…

April 2020, at my house in Sapporo
I was spreading a yoga mat in the living room and working hard on push-ups. I had no idea why I was doing this and where I was heading. But I needed to do something in order to hold on to myself. We were all obligated to avoid going outside under the slogan "stay home."
All right…
Before we get into the main story, let me briefly introduce myself.
I am Takeshi Kodama, forty-seven years old.
Profession: skier.
Hobby: skiing.
I was so into skiing when I was in college, I decided to devote all my energy into skiing for just two years after graduation. I thought I would be satisfied,

but after those two years of dedication, I realized the endless charm of skiing and made up my mind to live on skiing alone, becoming a self-proclaimed "professional skier." When I was young, I would ski on cliffs and unprecedented slopes. I spent a lot of my time flying around the world on expeditions. I was lucky enough to survive all the adventures, got married, and was blessed with children. However, I have always had the ambition to spend my lifetime skiing on snowy mountains around the world. That is what motivated me to start this "Ride the Earth" tour with Key Sato (forty-nine years old, professional photographer whose hobby is "camera").
I plan to continue this project until I am ninety years old, so long as I can still walk and enjoy the snowy mountains of the world. This is me.
I am happy when I am just skiing, but I am more than happy because sharing my ski experiences and excitement makes ski fans happy. Yes, I am a lucky guy.
There are many things to worry about, such as the political situations in related countries such as neighboring countries and environmental issues like global warming, but it was up to me to continue skiing, until all values were overturned by COVID-19.
First, all of my planned schedule was canceled. Not only me, but the whole ski industry was in a state of self-restraint.
Second, I went out to the mountains saying, "Skiing is the best way to

maintain good health because we can keep a safe distance while skiing."
Then, people starting to think going into the mountains was a social evil. "No way—if you get injured in the mountains, it will be big trouble. We are facing a medical care breakdown now!"
Then, I realized that without skiing, I was a 47-year-old man without a job who had never worked in an office.
"Oh, I have a serious issue."
What I had believed in was about to turn upside down.

"It might be difficult to go overseas and continue our project…"
I was talking to Key on the phone.
This project had started from Lebanon, then Morocco, Iceland, Kashmir, Russia, Greece, and China. We had traveled many times, but due to the global coronavirus pandemic, we were forced to cancel our eighth trip.
I have a folder named "Candidates for Ride the Earth" on my laptop. There are many pieces of information stored about the countries where we can ski. The stored information contains so many countries, if I went to one country a year, theoretically I could not complete the list of countries in my whole life, even if I continued this project and skied until I was ninety. Therefore, I was very serious about our opportunity given once a year this ski trip for this project since we both schedule conflicts.

スクワット…と毎日繰り返し鍛え上げてきた肉体が、巣立ちを迎えた鳥のように疼いている。頬を撫でる風の感触、土や草木の甘い香り、澄み渡った青い空を見上げながら、率直に思った。
「自然はコロナ以前より生き生きとしているじゃないか」
まるで何かを失ったかのように落ち込んでいた心に、涼しいそよ風が吹き抜けていくようだった。それからというもの、俺は何かに取り憑かれたかのように、自然の中に身をおく生活をおくるようになった。トレランで土や葉や草の感触を楽しみ、MTBでは風を楽しんだ。SUPでは海、湖、川を廻り、世界を繋いで巡る水の物語に耳を澄ませた。そして、確信してしまった。
「なんてこった。北海道ってスゲえよ…」
コロナ禍で海外に出られない現実を突きつけられた時、翼をもがれた鳥のような気分だったけれど、俺は、何をそんなに悲観的になっていたんだ？　何もかもあるじゃないか。ないものを探す方が難しかったのだ。
そう思っていた折、圭くんから電話が入った。
圭くん「今年も地球を滑る旅、やろう！」
俺「もしかして、同じこと考えていた？」

地球を滑る旅を続けてきた俺たちだからこそ、北海道を俯瞰して、本当の魅力に迫れるのではないだろうか？　そこで目をつけたのが、俺的に世界一の雪を誇るエリアだと思っている大雪山を中心とした広域の粉雪圏だった。ニセコや白馬など、いくつかの大きなスキー場やバックカントリーエリアが集まってブランド化された地域に比べ、大雪山自体に大きなスキー場があるわけではなく、トマム、富良野、カムイ、旭岳、黒岳など、かなり広域に渡ってスキー場が点在しているため、ぼんやりと「雪が良い地域」というイメージで、エリアとしてのブランド力が弱かった。その現状を「もったいないな〜」と思っていたのが、元月刊スキージャーナルの編集長で、現在中富良野にて「ノーザンスターロッジ」を営んでいる加藤雅明さんだ。仕事で世界中のスキー場を飛び回っていた加藤さんが感心したのは、カナダの内陸にあるパウダートライアングルだ。パウダースノーに恵まれた３つのスキー場、ファーニー、レッドマウンテン、ホワイトウォーターは、バンフやウィスラー・ブラッコムといった世界的なリゾートの陰に完全に隠れてしまっていた。しかし、パウダートライアングルと名付けられたことがきっかけで、世界中からパウダースノーフリークが集まるようになったのだ。これをヒントに加藤さんが6年ほど前に提唱したのが「北海道パウダーベルト」だ。

「北海道パウダーベルトを1シーズンかけて滑るなんてどうかな…」
圭くんが愛してやまないこのエリアを1冊の本にまとめるのは、圭くん自身としては近い将来にやりたいと思っていたことだったし、地球を滑る旅としても、いずれは地元「北海道」をやろうと考えていた。コロナによってその時期が早まっただけのことだ。それは海外に行けないから地元で…ということではなく、本当にやりたかったことだった。

But given the current situation, there was no way that we could travel and go abroad and continue the project as we used to do.

Now, looking at my empty schedule, I remembered when I was in my early twenties, skiing every day without any doubt, focusing on my performance. I became a professional skier because I love skiing. But thinking back, for a few years I had been too busy to immerse myself in my skiing.

I needed to stay positive and creative.
I turned off the television, took distance from my cell phone. Then, I had time to read books slowly. And more than enough time to do push-ups, abdominal crunches, chin-ups, and squats… My body was trained repeatedly every day, making me feel like now I was ready to fly out like a young fledgling bird. I vividly felt the wind stroking my cheeks and enjoyed the sweet scent of grass and soil. Looking up to the clear blue sky, I thought, "Nature is livelier than it was before the corona pandemic."
It was like a fresh cool wind in my depressed heart, as if I had lost something when the pandemic occurred. After this, I indulged in nature as if I was obsessed. I enjoyed the feel and touch of soil, leaves, and grass when I ran the trials. MTB (mountain bicycling) was joyful with winds. SUP (stand up paddle boarding) allowed me to have fun around the sea, lakes, and

rivers, listening to the stories of the water that connects the world.
And I concluded, "What the hell, Hokkaido is amazing!"
When I faced my inability to travel abroad due to this pandemic, I felt like a bird that had lost his wings. Now, I realize there is no reason to be pessimistic. Everything that I need is here, here in Hokkaido. It is hard to find what is missing here!
When I was thinking about this and that, my phone started to ring.
Key: "Let's continue the project this year!"
Takeshi: "Are we thinking the same thing?"
We had been together in this project, "Ride the Earth," for quite some time, and had traveled to so many countries, we would be able to explore the real charm of Hokkaido with a bird's-eye view. Yes, we now had big wings to fly.

Now the target was settled. But Hokkaido is a huge area for skiing/snowboarding, so we wanted to focus on the area that we considered the best of the best, which was the wide powder snow area surrounding Daisetsuzan (Mt. Daisetsu). Contrary to the several well-branded resort areas and backcountry areas like Niseko or Hakuba, Daisetsuzan doesn't have a big ski resort but several nice ski slopes. Tomamu, Furano, Kamui, Asahidake, and Kurodake are widely dotted across this area. No specific name had been given to this area; we just had a vague impression of the

image of an "area with good snow."
Mr. Masaaki Kato, former editor-in-chief of Ski Journal magazine, now owner of the Northern Star Lodge in Naka-Furano, always spoke highly and understood the value of this area. "This area should be branded!"
He had wide experience and knowledge of many ski slopes and snow resorts around the globe. One of the areas that he had been deeply impressed with was the Powder Triangle, in inland Canada. Three ski areas, Fernie, Red Mountain, and Whitewater, were in the shade of well-known worldwide resorts, Banff and Whistler-Blackcomb. But they were brought to light by being named the "Powder Triangle," and many powder snow freaks from around the world started to visit there.
With this fact, Mr. Kato proposed the "Hokkaido Powder Belt" six years ago.
Key said, "How about using the whole season to explore the Hokkaido powder belt?"
Making a book about this area was something that Key wanted to do in the near future, since he loved this area very much. At some point when the time comes, we were also thinking about focusing our project on our local Hokkaido.
The corona pandemic just made it earlier. It's not just that we had no way to travel abroad and our only option was to do it here. This was what we had really wanted to do for a long time.

気が早いシーズンイン 安政火口、富良野スキー場

大雪山には、当然4つの季節がある。長い冬と、ゆっくり訪れる春。一斉に訪れる夏と、束の間の秋だ。木枯らしが吹き抜ける頃、同時に雪が舞い降りる。大雪山の秋は、本当に短いのだ。

俺たちを乗せたJeep Wranglerは、落ち葉を巻き上げながら十勝岳連峰の裾野を颯爽と駆け抜けていく。山々の上部がうっすらと白くなった程度なので、滑るには気が早過ぎるのはわかっていた。しかし、俺のスキー欲求は沸点を優に超え、熱しすぎたフライパンのように煙を上げていた。先シーズンはコロナ禍によって4月でブツッと強制終了し、その後も外出すら満足にできない状況を経て、狂おしいほどにスキーが大好きだということを再確認してしまった。コロナは皮肉にも、ただ長生きすることよりも、楽しい時間を過ごすことの方がずっと重要ということを気付かせてくれたのだ。

さて、今まで7回に渡って世界中を滑ってきた「地球を滑る旅」は、3週間という短期間で偶然の出会いを求める旅だった。でも、今回の舞台は地元北海道ということで、今までとは違うことを企んでいた。それは、初雪から雪解けまでの雪の季節を旅すること。そして、様々なスキーヤー・スノーボーダーと滑ることで、感じることの違いを楽しむことだ。そこで、最初のライディングパートナーとして圭くんが声をかけたのが、中富良野在住のスノーボーダー、浅川雄介だった。

雄介はインドの修行僧のような怪しい風貌と、ミスマッチな物腰の柔らかさで、なんだか癖になるキャラだ。それにしても、スノーボーダーの握手は、何故、フワッと緩いのだろうか。これは俺の偏見かもしれないが、特にネイチャー系のスノーボーダーは得てして握手が弱く声が小さい。控えめな性格の人が多く、バリバリ自己主張するタイプの人は稀のような気がする。一方、スキーヤーは握手が強くて声がでかく、自己主張が強いタイプが多いような気がする。

雄介は、そのヒッピー的な風貌こそインパクト大だが、自然に対しても、人に対してもさりげなく優しい生き方をしているように見える。圭くんと出会ってから、雄介のようなライフスタイルスノーボーダーと滑る機会が多くなり、俺はその時間を楽しみにしていた。

十勝岳温泉の凌雲閣の駐車場に到着すると、濃霧が山全体を包み込んでいた。このような天気でも、澄み渡ったピーカンでも、雄介の態度は変わらない。表面的なことに一喜一憂しない雄介の一貫した態度は、山での時間を過ごす時、とても心地よく感じられた。一向に濃霧が切れそうにないので、駄目もとで安政火口方面に向かうことにした。ハイシーズンではありえないくらい準備の手際が悪いけど、そんなおぼつかなさも含めて、俺たちは、初滑りという儀式を楽しもうとしていた。まだ積雪が不十分なのでハイマツが剥き出しになって

いて、登山道を忠実に登っていかなければならなかった。俺は、生まれたばかりの赤ん坊を愛でるような気持ちで、一歩一歩雪を踏みしめながら、初雪を待ちながら過ごした季節に想いを馳せていた。春紅葉の時期、山菜を探した里山の空気。夏真っ盛りの山を駆け上がり、大汗をかいて寝そべった岩にひょっこりと現れたカナヘビの姿。落ち葉が深く積もった登山道を、パウダースノーを滑るように駆け下りた10月の定山渓。空から、空気から、生き物から、俺は季節を感じ取り、日めくりカレンダーをめくるが如く、ゆっくりと季節が移ろいゆくのを楽しんでいた。そして、待ち望んでいた季節がやってくる。スキーヤーにとって、初雪は3回訪れる。1回目は、空からヒラヒラと雪片が舞う初雪。2回目は、辺り一面を一晩にして真っ白に包んでしまう初雪。そして、3回目は初滑りの日、スキーで感じる初雪だ。

身体の動きと、呼吸と、自然とが、ちょうどよくシンクロするリズムを意識しながら、巣立ちの雛がゆっくりと羽を広げるように、一歩一歩進んでゆく。山全体をうっすらと包んだ雪は、当然まだ十分な量とは言えず、ハイマツや笹の質感が山肌にくっきりと残っていた。呼吸を落ち着かせ、鼓動に耳を澄ます。グローブのリスト部分を締め直し、ポールのストラップに手を通しながら、山全体を見渡す。ゴーグルを

Quite Early in the Season Ansei crater, Furano Ski resort

Our Jeep Wrangler dashed along the road of the Tokachi mountain range, rolling up the fallen leaves. We could see the thin white snow at the top of the mountains. We all knew it was way too early to ski, but I could not hold in my desire to ski—my passion was starting to boil over, just like a pot that is overheated. Last season had been forced to terminate in April due to COVID-19. After that, I couldn't go out for a certain period; then I reaffirmed that I love skiing with all of my heart. I just could not hold myself back any longer.

For the past seven of our "Ride the Earth" projects, when we were enjoying snowy mountains around the world, it was approximately three weeks' short journey to seek a chance encounter. But this time, since the location would be our Hokkaido, we were seeking something different. Using our home advantage, we continued our journey from the beginning of the first snowfall to the thaw—the whole snow season. And we wanted to expose a wide range of skiers and snowboarders, enjoying various moments of gifts brought by snow.

Yusuke Asakawa—Key picked him as the first rider to join us.
Yusuke is a snowboarder who lives in Naka-Furano. His appearance was suspicious and he looks like an Indian monk, but his soft demeanor made

him very attractive and added complexity to his character, just like a peanut butter and jelly sandwich you would like to taste quite frequently.

His appearance might give you a shock, but he was always kind and generous to both nature and people, I think. Since I got to know Key, I've had many chances to have fun with riders like Yusuke, and I always look forward to these chances.

When we arrived at the parking lot of Tokachi Hot Spring, thick fog wrapped the entire mountain. Yusuke's attitude was never changed by this kind of factor, bad weather or clear blue sky. I felt very comfortable in the mountains with his calm attitude, never influenced by the small things.

We found that this thick fog would not go away, so we decided to change the location to Ansei Crater.

In the high season, we would be much maturer and smarter, but today was the first day of the season. We were even enjoying our additional time consumed for preparation and facing our first ritual of the season. We did not have enough snow at this time—the creeping pines (Pinus pumila) and bamboo were still not covered—so we were forced to follow the mountain trail. But I was feeling the happiness of being with a newborn baby who would give me great joy, and we walked up the trail one by one with pleasure.

As I climbed up, I was thinking of the time when I was waiting for this first snow. And how much I had been longing for the snow. Feeling nature, and fine-tuning my breathing and movement to synchronize with my whole surroundings. Just like a young bird trying to spread his wings in preparing to fly, I was moving my legs forward one by one. When we reached the drop point, I told myself to be calm and listen to my heartbeat. Tightened the wrist part of my gloves. Overlooking the entire mountain, I put my wrists through the straps of the poles. I set my goggles and took a deep breath. Then, as always, I waited for the signal to start from somewhere above, just like God's revelation.

Since we did not have enough snow, I tried to be soft and slide the skis, only stroking the surface. With this condition, I could not give a full performance. This may sound odd, but this incompleteness would make this first ski unforgettable and adorable.

Takeshi: "Now it's started."
Yusuke: "Yes, it has."
No other words came out of my mouth.
I just wanted to enjoy my happiness that my season had started now.

I could not stop myself from going to Furano Ski Resort, which would open

セットしながら大きく深呼吸する。そうしていると、スタートの合図は空から降りてくるのだ。雪の下に優しく、表面だけを撫でるようにスキーを滑らせていくが、やっぱりこの状況では、自分が満足いくようなパフォーマンスはできない。でも、だからこそ初滑りというのは、なんとも言い難いくらい愛おしいのだ。
俺「いよいよ始まったね…」
雄介「そうっすね…」
それ以上に言葉が出てこなかった。ただ、これから始まる冬の空気を感じながら、じわじわとこみ上げてくる歓びに浸っていた。

数日後、オープンする富良野スキー場が気になりすぎて、気がついたら足が向かっていた。雪山という夢のような場所を、老若男女、誰もが安全に楽しむことができるスキー場は、どんなテーマパークより夢のある場所だと思っている。スキーが大好きな人が集まったスキー場には、とにかく気持ち良いエネルギーが集まっているのだ。
「やっぱりスキーは永遠に不滅だな〜」
そんなことをしみじみ思っていると、キレキレの滑りを見せるスキーヤーに遭遇した。只者ではないと思ったけれど、それもそのはず。彼は、現役医大生でありながら、気狂いじみたスキー好きが高じて

スキー技術を研磨しまくり、今年の全日本スキー技術選手権大会で「あわや優勝か？」というところまで頭角を現した山野井全だった。もし彼が優勝したら、史上初の現役医大生で車の免許を持っていないチャンピオンになるので、大いに期待していたけれど、案の定（？）最終日にミスって首位から陥落し、結果5位でフィニッシュとなったのであった。
「無駄に元気良くていいね〜」とベテランらしく目を細めて見ていると、今度は風格のあるスキーヤーが現れた。長年、一緒に「雪育」というスキーの振興活動に取り組んでいる同志であり、日本を代表するスキーヤーとして活躍を続けている井山敬介だった。二人とも、それぞれのYouTubeチャンネルの撮影中で、面白いやりとりが雪上で繰り広げられた。特に約束しなくても、気の合う仲間に出会えることこそが、スキー場の最大の利点なのかもしれない。スキー場はコロナ対策バッチリで、緊張しながら営業している感じだけど、それでも頑張って営業してくれていることが嬉しかったし、雪上には変わらず笑顔や笑い声があることが嬉しかった。俺は、この1日をより鮮明に記憶（記録）に残したくて、あえてマスク着用で滑走するシーンを撮影して遊んだ。今日は、自分にとってスキーとは何かをじっくり考えて、再びスキー場に帰ってきた日であり、スキー場も大きな不安

を抱えながらも、歩み始めた1日である。この1日をしっかり胸に刻んでおこう。
スキー場から富良野市街を一望することができた。山の上から見ると街の規模は小さく、盆地に広がる農地と、それをグルリと取り囲む山々のスケール感に圧倒される。まだ緑を残した畑の表面にうっすらと雪が降り積もっている。本格的な冬が訪れる直前に、ほんの一瞬だけ見ることができる景色を目に焼き付けていた。

in a few days.
A ski resort where everyone, young or old, can safely enjoy is a kind of dreamlike place of snowy mountains. It's more of a dream place than any other theme park for me. A snow resort full of people who love skiing is full of positive energy. I was thinking, "After all, skiing is forever immortal."

Then I ran into a skier with super technique. He was not just a skier, he was a medical student who loved skiing, and with his love he was brushing up on his skiing skills; then, he was about to claim his victory in the All Japan Ski Technical Championship (basic ski) this year. If he won the championship, he would be the first champion who was a medical student without a driving license. I was really looking forward to seeing his victory, but on the last day, his crown fell off, and he finished fifth in the competition as expected.
"It's good to see a young man with useless energy."
I was gazing at him with my experienced eyes, and then here came the sophisticated and mature skier.
He was Keisuke Iyama, one of the best skiers in Japan, who had worked with me for years on our "yuki-iku" (snow education) activities.
They were here for a YouTube shoot, and a very interesting exchange was going on. What I like about the ski slope is that I can easily encounter my mates without any prior reservation.

The ski resort was very cautious about the pandemic, and they were taking all the preventive actions they could and running their facility quite nervously. I was so happy that they had opened their facility for us and continued their service. It was great to see people enjoy the snow with happy smiles and laughter, as it used to be. I wanted to remember this day very clearly (also in my record), so I decided to wear a mask during this day's session. This day was the day that I was back on the ski slopes after I had spent so many hours seeking what skiing meant to me. And also, the day that the ski resort restarted their service with unpredictable risks.
I wanted to remember this day.
From the ski slope, I could overlook all the city of Furano. From the peak, the city was so small, and farmland spread through the valley. I was overwhelmed by the huge scale of the mountains surrounding the valley. I could still see the green of the fields slightly covered by white snow.
I was deeply impressed by the scenery that I could see for only a moment, only just before the arrival of full-scale winter.

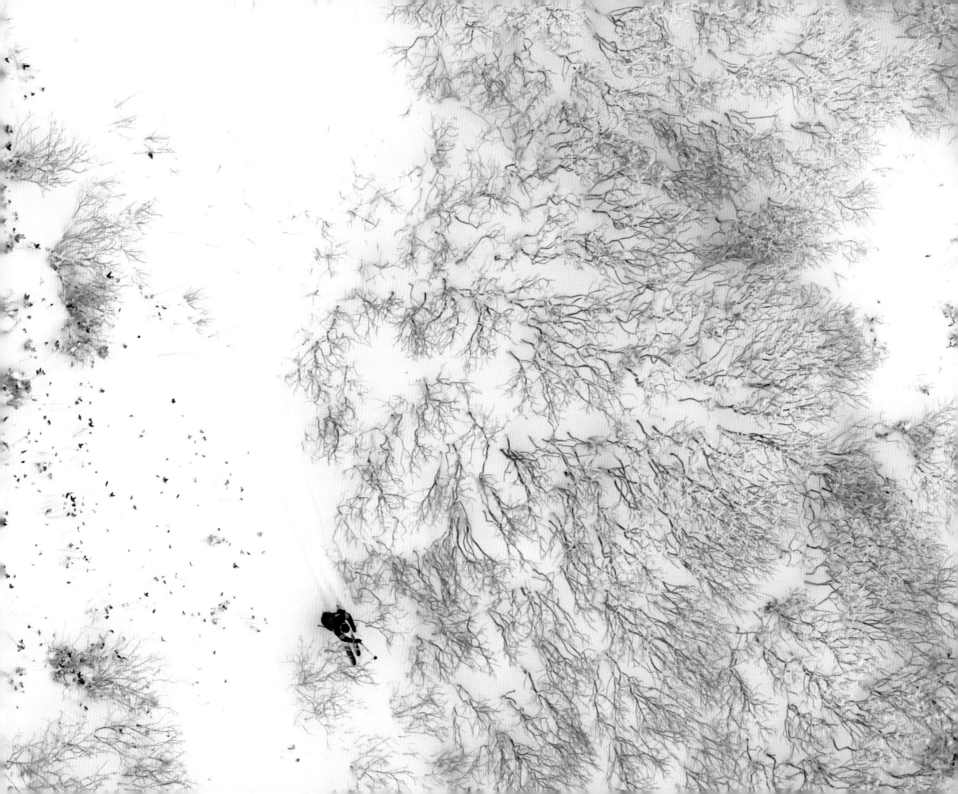

Yuusuke Asakawa

Zen Ymanoi

Keisuke Iyama

LOVE SKI HOKKAIDO トマム

「ギリギリ間に合った〜」
夜のトマムリゾート。レストランのニニヌプリが閉店する直前に滑り込んだ俺と圭くんは、北海道発のスキーTV番組「LOVE SKI HOKKADIO」の撮影班に合流したのだった。レストランの奥にいるのは、ひときわデカい男。彼は過去4回オリンピックに出場し、スラローム競技のワールドカップで日本人として過去最高の結果（2位3回）を残した伝説的なスキーヤー。現在日本のスキーシーンを先頭で引っ張るプロスキーヤー佐々木明だ。
「おお〜! タケさん、元気でしたか〜？!」
いつも変わらないハイテンションと笑顔。まさに、日本スキー界の太陽というにふさわしい。そしてもう一人は、前出の井山敬介。長年基礎スキーのトップ選手として活躍しながら、地元北海道の様々なTV番組で知名度を上げ、お茶の間の人気者にまでなっている。二人の大きな柱でやっているこの番組だが、実は立ち上げの時、俺も関わってきた経緯がある。冬のスケジュールが忙しく3年前にメインスキーヤーを退いたが、敬介と明は今もなお「雪育」という活動を共にする仲間なのだ。
敬介と初めて会ったのは2006年、スキー用品の展示会でのことだった。全日本スキー技術選手権大会での表彰台を射程圏内に捉え

勢いに乗っていた敬介のことは、人伝には聞いていた。その噂のスキーヤーが突然俺に話しかけてきたのだ。
「児玉毅さんですよね？ iconシリーズ(DVD)見てました！ 今度、一緒に滑ってもらえませんか？」
デッカイ笑顔で情熱的に語る敬介に、ちょっと圧倒されながら、その気持ちが嬉しくて、即座に「行こう！」と応えていた。そんな敬介の勢いに巻き込まれるようにして、あらゆるバックカントリーエリアでスキー撮影を重ね、基礎スキーとバックカントリースキーを融合したDVDをリリース。いつしか二人は「スキー界を盛り上げたい」という共通の夢を語るようになっていった。当時の敬介は造園屋のアルバイトを辞めてプロスキーヤー1本で食っていく覚悟をした1年目だった。プロスキーヤーとしてずっとやっていきたいと考えていた俺たちにとって、自分たちがスキー業界のみならず一般層に認知されることも大切だけど、もっと大切なことがあることに気づいていた。一時は1,800万人を数えた日本のスキー人口も、バブル崩壊後は減少の一途を辿り、スキー場も少しずつ減っていった。そして、北海道新聞の一面に載っていた記事が俺たちに衝撃を与えた。『かつて100%だった札幌市のスキー学習の実施率が30%にまで落ち込む』小中学校の授業数が減ったこと（ゆとり教育）に伴い、多くの中学校

がスキー学習を諦めたというのだ。
「ありえない！！」
世界でも稀に見る恵まれたスキー環境を生かし、昔から札幌の小中学生全員がスキー学習を経験してきたのだ。世界中のスキーヤーが羨むこの授業を、「授業数が足りない」という理由だけで、無くしてよいものだろうか？ いや、絶対にダメだ！
「これからスキーを盛り上げていくぜ！」という野望に水を差された格好になった俺と敬介は、「この問題をどうにかしなければ」と、週7という頻度で居酒屋に集まり、ビールを浴びるように飲みながら熱い議論を交わし続けた。その席で良いアイディアもチラホラ出ていたと思うが、酔っ払っているので翌日には綺麗さっぱり忘れている。学習能力に乏しい俺たちは、ミーティングという名の飲み会を繰り返しながら、ただ時間だけが過ぎていった。そんなある日のこと、この異様に熱いミーティングにたまたま参加したのが、昔からのスキーの友人である森脇俊文だった。彼は俺たちの戯言を丁寧にメモをとってくれ、その議事録（？）を起こして、酔いが覚めた俺たちに共有してくれるようになった。森脇のお陰で話し合いは前に進むようになり、俺たちは、あるアクションを起こすことを決心した。
「自分たちの大好きなスキーを守るために何ができるのかを話し

LOVE SKI HOKKAIDO TOMAMU

"Just in time!"
Tomamu Resort at night. Key and I made it just before the restaurant Nininupuri closed. We were planning to join the crew of the TV program, "LOVE SKI HOKKAIDO."
One was the muscular guy who was sitting in the back of the restaurant. He was a legendary skier who had participated in four Olympic Games and recorded the best result ever for a Japanese at the World Cup slalom competition (three times in second place). He was Akira Sasaki, a professional skier who is currently leading the Japanese ski scene.
Akira: "Hi Take-san, how's it going?"
Hyper and with a big smile as usual, I named him Mr. Sunshine.
The other was Keisuke Iyama. He had competed in the national basic ski competition as a top athlete for quite a long time, and he had become a popular figure, appearing on various TV programs in his hometown of Hokkaido.
Now, both of them were the main two pillars of the program. I had been deeply involved in the early stage of the program as one of the main cast. Since my winter schedule was so full, I couldn't remain as a main skier on the program three years ago, but both Keisuke and Akira were my companions and coworkers in the activity of "yuki-iku" (snow education).

When I first met Keisuke, it was in 2006 at the ski equipment exhibition. I had heard that he would be the next to stand on the podium at the All Japan Ski Technical Championship.
Keisuke said, "Hi, you must be Mr. Takeshi Kodama. I've watched the DVDs you were in! It would be great if I had a chance to ski with you."
A big smile on his face, he asked me full of passion. I was bit overwhelmed but replied to him instantly. I was happy that he had asked me to ski with him. "Yes, let's go!"
I got caught up in Keisuke's strong momentum; then we had a shooting session together in the field; then we released a DVD, a fusion of basic skiing and backcountry skiing.
We were starting to share the aspiration together to "revitalize the ski industry."
At that time, Keisuke had just quit his part-time job at a landscaping contractor, and it was his first year he had decided to live as a professional skier.
We are both continuing to live as professional skiers, but the reality is harsh. Japan's ski population, which at one time reached eighteen million, but after the bubble economy ended, the numbers dropped, and the number of snow resorts slowly decreased. One day, both of us were shocked by the article on the front page of Hokkaido Newspaper.

"The implementation rate of ski learning in Sapporo, which used to be 100%, drops to 30%."
Many junior high schools had given up on skiing, as the number of classes had decreased. (The new education initiative known as Yutori-Kyoiku was designed to relieve the pressure on students by reducing class hours and learning content for both elementary school and junior high school. Ski classes were easy to eliminate from the curriculum for junior high schools; therefore, for junior high schools, the percentage of students in ski class had dropped to only 30 percent.)
"This is not acceptable!" we both screamed.
Taking advantage of a blessed ski environment rarely seen in the world, all the elementary and junior high school students in Sapporo had been learning to ski in school.
All the skiers in this world envy this school learning, and it is not right to extinguish this rare class just because we do not have enough classes. This is not right! We need to do something!!!
We started to gather at Izakaya (casual restaurant where you can drink) seven times a week to brainstorm and discuss over so many beers.
We got so many good ideas over drinks, but we both were too drunk and forgot about them on the next day.
One day, Moriwaki, one of my old ski friends, joined this Izakaya discussion

合える場を設けよう！」

こうして、3回に渡って「スノースポーツミーティング」が開催された。決して派手ではないイベントだが、スキー業界の様々な立場の参加者が多いときで200名にものぼり、熱いブレーンストーミングが交わされた。その後、頭より情熱で動く俺たちらしく、みんなが提案してくれたアイディアを手当たり次第に実践したのだ。プロスキーヤーがスキー学習をジャックするスーパースキー学習は、とにかく楽しいスキー学習が子供たちにどのような影響を与えるかの実験だった。それによりプロスキーヤーによるスキー学習のための事前学習が効果的だという結論に至り、今も「雪育せんせいキャラバン」という出前授業として続いている。また、子供たちにスキーを教える先生方がスキーを好きでなければ、スキーの魅力は絶対に伝わらないと思い、先生方にスキーが大好きになってもらう「スーパースキー研修」を毎年実施。

これらの活動から「雪育」という言葉が生まれ、札幌市や地方自治体が協力する雪育イベントの開催や、札幌市の小中学校に配布する雪育のDVD教材作成に発展した。そのような様々な活動を経て、LOVE SKI HOKKAIDO という番組がスタートすることになったのだ。

and started to take minutes about each of the ideas popping up over beer, and he shared them with us when we were not influenced by alcohol.

This note-taking was a game-changer. Our discussion started to be productive, and we finally decided to take action.

"Let's set up a place to discuss what we can do to protect our favorite skiing!"

We had this "snow sports meeting" three times.

It wasn't a fancy event, but there were many participants, with various kinds of people in the ski industry involved. Some days there were over two hundred people, and heated exchanges of opinion occurred. After such productive meetings, the actions we took really represented ourselves. We carried out the entire proposal we received and put it into action.

"Super Ski Class": Professional skiers took over the class from teachers. This was an experiment to understand what kind of influence a super-fun skiing class can have. As a result of this, we found it would be more effective to have a pre-class session facilitated by professional skiers. We still continue this pre-class before the season as "yuki-iku delivery classes."

"Super Ski Training": We also concluded that teachers who give ski lessons to kids need to love skiing. Teachers are the ones who out create the fun and excitement—otherwise, how can kids be attracted to or recognize the charm of skiing? Therefore, we started training teachers to become huge lovers of skiing, and we are still offering this training every year.

With these activities, the word "yuki-iku" (snow education) was born.

Holding snow education events in cooperation with Sapporo city and local governments evolved into the creation of DVD teaching materials for snow education to be distributed to elementary and junior high schools in Sapporo.

After we were involved in these various "yuki-iku" (snow education) activities, this TV program called "LOVE SKI HOKKAIDO" started.

朝一のゴンドラを降り、撮影班が真っ先に向かったコースは、その名も「NO GRAVITY」。なんと秀逸なネーミングなのだろうか。POWDERという言葉を安易に使わず、その滑走感覚を表す抽象的な表現「無重力」が逆に想像力を掻き立て、なんとなく「宇宙的な」素敵な世界観を醸し出している。そんな意味深なコース名は少なくて、よくあるのが「ファミリーコース」「パノラマコース」。下手すると「Aコース」や「Bコース」といった感じだ。俺は、改めてスキーコースの名前は意外と大切だな〜と思うのだった。コースの全面を30cmほどの新雪が包み込み、幅広の急斜面が真っ直ぐフォールラインに向かい延々と続いていた。

「最初はグー、ジャンケンポン！」お決まりのジャンケンでスタート順を決める。撮影であり遊びである。このテンションの高さも、別にカメラが回っているからではない。とにかくパワフルに元気よく滑り、思いっきりリアクションし、大いに笑う。スキーが大好きなメンバーだからこそ、この番組の雰囲気が出来上がったのだ。まずは敬介がスピードをつけてジャンプしながら斜面に飛び込んでいった。初めて敬介と一緒にパウダースノーを滑った12年前は、基礎スキーらしい丁寧な滑りをしていたけど、今となっては、様々なターンやトリックを織り交ぜ、時にはあえて形を崩したりしながら、見るものを魅了する滑りだ。イメージする滑りを体現する能力に優れ、俺と明の間では、日本で一番スキーが上手いのは敬介じゃないかと話している。

明は、普通に滑れば誰よりも速く、誰よりもシャープで、誰よりもダイナミックなのに、型というものが何も存在しない自由な滑りをしてくる。長年、最もシビアなアルペンレースの世界でやってきて、どうしたらこんなにフリーなマインドになるのだろうか。スキーのエッジを全て取り払ってエッジレススキーにしたり、エッジレスを生かした全く新しい動きを編み出したり…。全てが予測不能で限りなくオリジナルなのだ。
「うわお！」「イェ〜！」「ナイス！！」「最高！！」スキーヤーもカメラマンも次々と発する叫び声。
それぞれの滑りに思いっきりリアクションすることが、何とも歯切れが良くて気持ちよかった。

広々としたスキー場を縦横無尽に遊び、雪まみれになった3人は、トマムの景観の代名詞でもあるツインタワーに向かって滑っていった。スキーインスキーアウトできる複合施設「ホタルストリート」でランチをとろうと思っていた。海外のリゾートでは、スキーをする人もしない人も関係なく冬になったら三世代でスキーリゾートを訪れる。スキーの楽しさや冬の山岳リゾートの美しい景観は言うまでもないけど、食事やショッピング、アクティビティなど、子供からお年寄りまで楽しめる要素がビッチリと詰まっている。トマムを経営する星野佳路さん曰く、スキー・スノーボードをしないファミリーも取り込むこと、

そして、夏にどれだけ利益をあげられる運営をするかが、スキー場が生き残る上で最大のポイントなのだ。
普段、バックカントリーエリアばかり滑っている俺にとって、宿泊型のリゾートスキーは何もかもが新鮮だ。トマムの取り組み一つ一つに愛情を感じ、トコトン非日常に浸れるリゾートづくりに感心し、自分自身が「夢の国」の住人になったような気分だった。
「こりゃあ、みんな楽しいわな」
自然と家族の顔が浮かび、みんなでトマムに訪れるイメージをしてワクワクしていた。

Back to Tomamu.
The name of the slope that the shooting team headed to after getting off the first gondola in the morning was "NO GRAVITY."
What an excellent name!
Without using POWDER, your imagination will be stimulated by abstract expression of GRAVITY. You can easily understand this slop will not be packed. The choice of the words generates an inspiring cosmic view.
It is rare to find this kind of meaningful poetic name. What's common is Course A or Course B. Encountering this fancy name made me think that the name of the ski course is surprisingly important.
It was covered with thirty centimeters of fresh snow, a wide steep slope straight toward the fall line, and I could not see the end from where I stood.
"Paper, rock, scissors!"
We decided the starting order in the usual way.
This was a shoot. At the same time, this was our time to have fun. This hyper excitement was not because we were being filmed. We skied powerfully, reacted to each other, and laughed a lot.
I love the atmosphere of this program. This can happen with the chemical reaction of super ski lovers.
First was Keisuke. He jumped off to the slope with high speed. Akira and I always said to each other, probably Keisuke was the best skier in Japan, with his excellent ability to embody what he imagined. Various turns and tricks with playful twists of unbalancing—his style would attract everyone.

Then Akira—he had been competing in Alpine skiing for years and should have become a boxier person. But I had never met anyone more open-minded than him. Skiing normally, he was faster, sharper, and more dynamic than anyone, but when we were having fun together, his style was free and open, and there were no rules or types in his skiing.
He was unpredictable and unique in everything!
He took out all the edges from skiing, made edge-less skiing, and played with this edge-less skiing and developed new motion.
The last one was me.
"Wow!", "Yeah!", "Nice!", "Amazing!"
Both performing skiers and camera crews could not hold in their voices. It was a joyful moment when we reacted to each other's performance and cheered each other on.
We were covered with snow from playing around the spacious ski area. Then we started to head to Tomamu's famous feature, the Twin Towers, to take lunch at Hotaru Street, which we could reach by skiing.
Whether you ski or not, all kinds of people visit ski resorts in winter, with three generations together in other countries. It is not only the fun of skiing or beautiful mountains covered with snow and the spectacular view from the resort, but the resorts are also packed with elements that people from children to the elderly can enjoy, such as good food, shopping, and various activities.

Yoshiharu Hoshino, CEO of Hoshino Resort, said that the most important point for a ski resort to survive is how profitable it is in the summer and how to incorporate families who do not ski or snowboard.
Since most of the time I skied in the backcountry field, an accommodation-type resort ski was totally fresh and interesting.
Moved by each of Tomamu's efforts, I was deeply impressed by the well-built resort where you could immerse yourself in an extraordinary life. I felt like I was staying in Dreamland.
"This is fun for everyone."
The faces of my family naturally came to my mind, and the image of visiting Tomamu together made me happy.

Keisuke Iyama

Akira Sasaki

日本のスキー文化 比布

最近、ローカルスキー場を巡っているスキーヤーが増えてきたような気がする。いわゆるリゾートスキー場があまりにも有名過ぎて、小さなスキー場は目立たないけれど、リゾートスキー場は10箇所もないのに対し、小さなスキー場100箇所以上あるのだ。その中には小さな丘にロープトーを架けただけの小規模スキー場もあるけれど、魅力的なローカルスキー場がいくつもある。北海道は広いだけに、スキー場からの眺めも、雰囲気も、ゲレ食も、全てが違って個性的。そんな魅力に敏感な人はちゃんといて、長年かけていろいろなスキーを一通り経験した人が、新たな楽しみ方を求めて密かにローカルスキー場をハシゴする旅をしているという。俺と同い年のプロスキーヤー浅川誠が、旭岳やカムイスキーリンクスを滑った後に、ローカルスキー場をハシゴするのが日課だと聞いた時、「変態だな…」と思ったものだが、この環境を知れば知るほどハシゴする意味が分かってくる。まず、旭川で言えば比布、和寒、サンタプレゼントパーク、キャンモア、伊ノ沢といったローカルスキー場があり、そのどれもが峠道のドライブを要さない平地に隣接している。つまり町からフラッと行って遊べる近さにあるのだ。そして、標高が低いのに雪質がドライで、圧雪バーンはナイターの時間になっても荒れておらず、適度にしまった状態を常にキープしている。雪が降った直後であれば、コース脇に

パウダースノーがクオリティーをそのままに残っている。そして、どのスキー場もリフト券が激安ときたもんだ。というわけで、俺たちも浅川に習って、軽くローカルスキー場巡りを試みることにした。

俺たちが訪れたのは、旭川の北に位置する「比布スキー場」。リフト券を買おうとセンターハウスに歩いて行くと、スキー置き場に並んでいるスキーは真っ白いカンダハースタイルの自衛隊スキーだけだった。北海道のスキー場では、自衛隊がスキー訓練をする姿は見慣れた光景になっている。ところで、たくさんの小さなスキー場が点在しているのは、世界的に見て珍しいことをご存知だろうか。海外のスキー場は、そのほとんどが宿泊施設を備えたリゾートだ。街から遠隔地にあるため宿泊を要することが多く、スキーバケーションなど長期にわたる休暇のスタイルもあるからだ。それに比べて、日本には小さなスキー場が多い。これらは明らかに地元のスキー普及を考えて意図的に増やしてきたスキー場なのだ。しかし、スキー場が増えるだけでスキーは普及するのだろうか？ お世辞にも魅力的とは言えない小規模スキー場でもみんな熱心にスキーに取り組んだのは、日本独自のスキー文化が起因している。剣道や柔道のように鍛錬を重ねて昇進していく「道」の世界をスキーにも取り入れたのだ。

そう。日本のスキーはレジャーというより「スキー道」の要素が強かったのだ。研究熱心で練習熱心な日本人は、スキーの達人になるべく、レッスンや研修を受け、検定などに取り組むようになった。爆発的にスキー人口が増えていくのを支えたのは、農閑期にスキー場で働く農業従事者をはじめとする季節労働者、冬休みなどに子供を指導する時間が取りやすい教職員、繁忙期の土日祝日に応援に駆けつけやすい公務員や会社員など…。結果、スキーを職業としないアマチュアが強い団体が実権を握るようになった。そして、日本の好景気と共にスキーブームを迎え、さらにスキーの普及は加速。スキー＝レジャー、レッスン＝サービスという概念をやや置き去りにしたまま膨張していった。そんな日本のスキー場が、バケーションで訪れる大勢の外国人に戸惑わない訳がない。日本人がオロオロしている間に外国人が参画してきて、外国人による外国人のためのスキーリゾートになってしまった例もあるのだ。

おそらく何十年も変わっていないシンプルな低速ペアリフトに乗って山頂に向かう。古いけれどしっかり整備され、大切に使われている施設なのが伝わってくる。本当に良いコースを滑るとコースが語りかけてくるのだ。この山に目をつけ、斜面を設定し、コースを敷いた人の

Japanese ski culture Pippu

Recently, I feel that the number of skiers visiting local ski resorts has increased. The big-name ski resorts are so famous that small ski resorts hide in their shadows. The number of big ski resorts is no more than ten, but there are more than a hundred small ski resorts. Many of them are small ski slopes with a rope tow on a hill, but you can find many attractive local small ski resorts. Since Hokkaido has a large area, the view from the ski resort, the atmosphere, and the food served there are all different and unique.
There are people who are sensitive to such charms. They enjoy exploring the unknown local small ski resort and travel to several resorts, ski-resort-hopping.
Makoto Asakawa is a professional skier who is the same age as me. When I first heard that he did this hopping after he enjoyed skiing at Asahidake or Kamui Ski-links, I first thought of him as a "way too eccentric skier," but the more I understand about the area, the keener I on why he hops resorts.
The first reason: in the Asahikawa area, there are so many small local snow resorts—Pippu, Wassamu, Santa Present Park, Canmore, and Inosawa. They are adjacent to flatlands that do not require a challenging drive over the mountain, pass and each of the resorts has easy access from the town.
Second, these snow resorts are gifted with dry snow though the altitude is low. Even in nighttime, packed snow slopes are preserved in good condition. When you have fresh snowfall, you can still enjoy the powder snow

remaining on the side of the course at night.
Moreover, at all of these snow resorts, you can buy a lift pass at a very inexpensive cost.
Therefore, we took Makoto Asakawa's tips and tried a light version of local ski-resort-hopping.

We visited Pippu Ski Resort, located north of Asahikawa.
When we tried to buy lift tickets at the ski center, all we could see in the ski yard was white cable binding-style skis, which the Self-Defense Forces use in their training. It is a familiar sight to see the Self-Defense Forces training for skiing in Hokkaido.
By the way, do you know that it is rare in the world that many small ski resorts are scattered around this area? Many of the overseas snow resorts have accommodation facilities, since they are far from cities and people therefore need to stay at the resorts. People stay at the resorts for long vacations, customized as ski vacations.
Contrary to overseas, in Japan we have many small snow slopes, as we have decent snowfall in the plains. These small ski slopes are built intentionally, aiming to popularize skiing. But do you think increasing the number of snow slopes would increase the population of skiers?
When the ski population burst, people worked hard on skiing, even at the

small snow slopes that are not so attractive, due to Japan's unique ski culture. Skiing was introduced with a promotion system, just like in kendo (swordsmanship) or judo. (When you get better in judo, you will get a black belt.) In Japan, somehow ski was twisted into a certification program than the joyful leisure which is the essence of skiing. Japanese are very enthusiastic about research and practice. They take lessons and training, aiming to become certified masters in skiing.
The explosive growth of the skiing population was supported by seasonal workers, including farmers who work at ski resorts during the off-season, teachers who can easily take time to teach children during their winter vacation, and public service workers and office workers who can easily come to support on weekends and holidays during the busy season. As a result, the ski industry was dominated by an organization mostly run by amateurs who were not specialized in skiing. With the booming economy in Japan, the ski boom began, and the spread of skiing accelerated and continue to inflate without a concept of Skiing = Leisure, or Lesson = Service.
When you understand our background, you can easily understand why most Japanese snow resorts couldn't handle the large numbers of foreigners visiting well. In fact, many foreign companies came in and built ski resorts for foreigners, by foreigners.

思いがある。少しでも楽しんでもらおうと丁寧に整備するオペレーター、安全管理するパトロール、索道の係員。そして、このスキー場を愛するファンの思いがコースに染み込んでいる。実際に滑ってみるとコースの長さに対する斜度がちょうどよく、綺麗な一枚バーンに見えて微妙にうねっているあたりがスキーヤーの興奮を呼び覚ます。圧雪の仕上がりが美しく、丹念に織り込まれた絹織物のようだ。そして、知る人ぞ知るパウダーコースやコブの練習レーンも…。
極め付けは、児玉毅が勝手に認定する日本のゲレ食10選にも選ばれたいくら丼とあら汁のセット600円! ベースには温浴施設もあると来たら、ファンがついている理由は十分に分かるだろう。海外では、スキーはもっとお金持ちの遊びで、アメリカのベイルなんかは1日券が2万円以上する。日本のように庶民でも気軽にスキーが楽しめる国は少ないのだ。アジア諸国が急速に経済発展を遂げ、その後にはアフリカが続こうとしている。このような雪国ではない地域でも、経済発展すれば必ずと言っていいほどスキーが流行ってきた。中国の人工雪スキー場が大混雑をしているような状況で、富裕層はどこに滑りにいくのか…。外国の人たちにも北海道の雪の素晴らしさを知ってもらいたい気持ちと、誰でもお手軽に、のんびり滑ることができた日本のスキー文化も大切にしたい気持ちとが、心の中で交錯していた。

We were heading to the peak, riding on the slow pair chairlift, which hadn't changed for decades. It was old, but I could tell it was well maintained and carefully used. And when you are skiing on a good slope, that the slope speaks to you the passion of the person who picked this mountain and set the slope and laid the course, or the operator who carefully maintains the equipment so that people can have fun, the patrol staff for safety management, the cableway staff. And all the passion of this snow resort's fans stays in the slope as a good vibe.

When I skied, the length and steepness were just right. It looked like a wide straight slope, but slightly undulating, requiring technique to enjoy, awakening my excitement.

The finishing touch of the compressed snow was beautiful, and it looked like carefully woven silk fabric.

We also enjoyed the powder course, well-known only to those in the know.

At the base town, you can enjoy hot springs; there is no reason for them not to be attached to this snow resort.

In some countries, skiing is a luxurious pleasure for the rich.

Lift chair tickets at the Vail Resort in the USA cost more than 180 US dollars per day. Japan is the rare country where you can enjoy skiing at an amount most common people can pay.

Asian countries started to develop their economies rapidly in the last century, and now Africa is getting on its way. Historically, skiing has become popular in every country where the economy has developed. We can easily know the answer to where the rich people in China will go to ski when China's artificial snow ski resort is very crowded. I was in antinomy: Did I want to cherish the Japanese ski culture that allowed everyone to ski and enjoy it without any rush? Or let foreigners know more about the wonderfulness of the snow in Hokkaido?

師匠を訪ねて カムイ

「おう、タケ」

カムイスキーリンクスに到着するや否や、初老の男性がスクールのプレハブから顔を出して言った。どんな時も肩の力が抜けた雰囲気で、誰にでも気さくに声をかけてくれる。この63歳の親父こそが、俺が最もお世話になったスキーヤーの一人である尾形信さんだ。尾形さんは、冒険スキーヤーの三浦雄一郎さん率いるスノードルフィンに入門してから、カムイ校 校長、テイネ校 副校長、再びカムイ校校長と歴任。スノードルフィンの黄金時代にトップスキーヤーとして活躍し、日本のフリースキーシーンの礎を築いた一人である。俺がスキーに取り組み始めた19歳の頃から、一番近くで成長を見守ってくれていたのが尾形さんだった。

19歳の秋、スキーインストラクターをやれば、バイトをしながらスキーが上手くなってあわよくばモテるかもしれない！ と思った俺は、リゾートというリゾートに履歴書を送った。しかし、下心を見抜かれたのか、どこのスクールにも受け入れてもらえず、唯一面接に漕ぎつけたのが、なんと冒険スキーヤーの三浦雄一郎さん率いるスノードルフィンだった。「すごいところに連絡しちゃった…」少し後悔しながら、スクールの事務所を訪れたのだが、事務員の一人が困った顔を

していた。面接官の副校長がどっかに行ったっきり帰ってこないというのだ。俺は、微妙な心境で応接間のソファーに座って待ち続け、1時間後にようやく現れたのが尾形副校長だった。「おお！ わりぃわりぃ！」ちょっと照れ笑いを浮かべている。どうやら遅刻したというよりは、すっかり忘れていたらしい。めちゃくちゃ緊張していたのがバカらしくなってきた。尾形さんは俺の目を一瞬チラッとみたかと思うと、正面のソファーに座るや否や一言、「採用」と言った。

「…はい？ 今なんて言いましたか？」

「採用するよ。うちは給料安いけど、いいよな？」

面接って、もうちょっと質問とか、いろいろあるんじゃないの？ もちろん給料は安くない方が良いけど、今はひとまずインストラクターとして拾ってもらえるだけでも嬉しかった。

そんなこんなでスノードルフィンに入門した俺だったが、そこで待っていたのは、軍隊映画も色褪せるスノードルフィン伝統の体育会系バリバリの世界だった。雑用の命令と宴会芸の命令以外に、先輩から声をかけられることがなかった中で、尾形さんはちょくちょく声をかけてくれた。

「タケ、ちょっとこっち来い」

「はい！」と喜んで歩み寄ると、

「なんだその滑り。ダッセ～なぁ」と言ったかと思うと、笑いながら滑っていってしまった。それでも、ほとんどの先輩に声さえかけてもらえなかった中で、尾形さんの一言はいつも辛口だけど「見てくれる人もいるんだ」と励みに感じていた。スノードルフィンにお世話になって4シーズンが経った頃、相変わらず尾形さんに褒められることはなかったけど、大学を卒業して全ての時間をスキーに注いでみたいと思っていた。アメリカに武者修行に出て自分の力を試してみたい。やる気だけは満タンの俺だったが、スクール繁忙期である1月中旬に旅立つことはヒンシュクものだった。そこで声をかけてくれたのが尾形さんだった。

「タケ、スクールの事は俺がなんとかフォローしておくから、心配しないでアメリカで思いっきり暴れてこい」

「あ…ありがとうございます！」

「スキーでどこまでやれるかトコトンやってみろ。いいか、俺は今まで数えきれないほど若いスキーヤーを見てきたが、大学を卒業後もスキーを続けてみると言ったのは、庄司克史（※）とオマエの二人だけだ」そう言って尾形さんは笑った。アメリカでのスキー武者修行から帰国した時、尾形さんは俺の滑りを見て、実に愉快そうに

（※）庄司克史、1990年代に日本のフリースキーのアイコンとして活躍。シーンに多大なる影響を与えた。

Visit the master Kamui

"Hi, Take."

As soon as I arrived at Kamui Ski-links, he found me and greeted me, coming out from the ski school office.

Makoto Ogata, a sixty-three-year-old good man who can talk to anyone in a relaxed atmosphere at any time.

He was one of the skiers that I was most indebted to. Mr. Ogata started his career by joining Snow-Dolphins, a famous ski school led by famous adventure skier Yuichiro Miura. He had served as Principal of Kamui, Deputy Principal of Teine, and Principal of Kamui again. He was one of the top skiers in the golden age, who laid the foundation of Japanese free skiing. He was one of my mentors who had closely watched my development and growth since I was nineteen.

I joined Snow-Dolphins when I was nineteen. There was a traditional Snow-Dolphin jock style stricter than military discipline. I was never called out by my seniors besides chore orders and party skit orders, but Mr. Ogata frequent talked to me like:

"Take, come up here."

And I ran to him with willingness. "Yes, Ogata-san!"

Then he said, "Why is it that you don't look cool when you ski? Hahaha."

And skied away down the slope with laughter.

Even so, while most of my seniors didn't even talk to me, Mr. Ogata encouraged me, as he was watching over me, though his words were always short and simple.

Four seasons after I had joined Snow-Dolphins, there was no particular word of appraisal from Mr. Ogata. But I was starting to think that after my graduation from college, I would spend all my time skiing. And I had ambition to go to the USA to test my strength and technique. My heart was on fire. Generally, graduation time in Japan is early March, meaning my departure would be after I took all the exams in the beginning of January, at the busiest time of the year for ski school, in mid-January, which everyone was upset about.

But Mr. Ogata said this:

"Take, do not worry about school. I will cover you. Go wild in the USA."

"Oh, thank you so much, sir!"

"Try and challenge yourself how far you can go. I ski with a lot of young skiers. You and Katsushi Shoji (※) are the only two whom I encourage to continue skiing after college." He said this with a big smile and a laugh.

After I was back from my adventure in the USA, Mr. Ogata assessed my skiing and said with joy:

"You are going do it [as a professional skier], right?"

This was first compliment out of his mouth, which made it my destiny to become a professional skier

After this event, Mr. Ogata was involved in my ski career highlight. During the Everest expedition, he came to support me for a month.

After so many years, now Mr. Ogata is in his sixties, but he still loves skiing, and he is on the slopes every day. Looking at his back, I always feel a sense of security together with him. I visit Kamui once a year and look forward to skiing with him.

Communication is important for skiers, and we can communicate something by skiing together. What we share when we ski together: the same slopes, the same scenery, and the same smile.

"Let's ski together."

There is a lot of content in these simple words.

Kamui has Mr. Ogata; if I want to ski with him, all I need is visit Kamui.

We drove to Furano on Route 38 with satisfaction. The sun was about to fall below the horizon, and we were colored in red by the setting sun.

(※) Katsushi Shoji, He played an active part by Japanese free ski industry in 1990 's. He had a great influence on the scene.

「やるんでしょ」と言った。尾形さんが俺に対して発した初めての褒め言葉。その一言で、俺はプロスキーヤーになることを決意したのだ。それからというもの、尾形さんは要所要所で声をかけてくれ、エベレスト遠征の時は、山行がスムーズに進むよう、1ヶ月間もサポートに来てくれたことがあった。

思い返せば、自分のスキー人生の大切な節目に、必ずと言っていいほど尾形さんの存在があった。それから年月が過ぎ、尾形さんは還暦を過ぎたけれど、今も変わらずスキーが大好きで、毎日雪上に立ち続けていた。その後ろ姿を見ると、なんとも言えない安心感に包まれるのだ。俺は、1年に1度はカムイを訪れ、尾形さんと滑るのを楽しみにしていた。

朝一のカムイスキーリンクスは、完璧に整備されたコースで迎えてくれた。スキー場の麓に大型のホテルがないので、どちらかというと市民スキー場的な雰囲気だけど、スキーエリアのポテンシャルにおいては、どんなリゾートにも引けをとっていない。つまり、ものすごく贅沢なスキー場というわけだ。
「とりあえず、ゴールドコースでも行ってみようか」
尾形さんは、一言ボソッと言ったかと思うと飄々と滑り始めた。63歳とは思えないハイスピードなので、気を抜いていると一気に離されてしまう。俺はギアを上げて尾形さんの後ろにピッタリとついた。
――やっぱりかっこいいな～
尾形さんの背中を追うたびに思う。完璧なポジションから生まれるリラックスしたスタイル。その動き一つ一つが洗練されていて、一片の無駄もない。尾形さんの背中を追いながら、15年前に他界した故・三浦敬三さんを思い出していた。敬三さんは、三浦雄一郎さんの父であり、日本スキー界の草分けであると同時に、100歳まで滑り続けたスキーの神様的な存在だ。敬三さんは、まさにリアルなスキー仙人だった。90歳を超えるような年齢になると、昨日できていたことが今日できなくなっているという、争うことのできない圧倒的な老いのスピードを感じることがあるという。それでも、スキーに寄せる情熱は少しも薄れることはなく、スキー用具のチューンナップを研究し、滑りの理論を研究し、ひたすら雪の上に立ち続けた。晩年は、

気が遠くなるくらいスキーの準備に時間がかかり、両ストックを杖のようにしてようやく雪の上に立っていた。それでも、一度スキーを履くと、突然何十歳も若返ったかのように風を切って滑り始めるのだ。「骨で滑る」と表現する究極の省エネ滑走術は圧巻で、俺はスキーの奥深さを目の当たりにした気がした。昔、拳法の達人である老人が、大男を指一突きで倒す映像を見たことがある。もしかしたら、敬三さんはそれに似た奥義に到達したスキー仙人なのかもしれない。敬三さんから派生したスキーの弟子、又弟子は数えきれず、日本各地、さらには世界各地に点在しているが、最も滑りを受け継いでいるのが尾形さんではないだろうか。スピードやパワーやパフォーマンスではない根本的な何かが尾形さんのスキーにはあるのだ。俺は、尾形さんの背中を追って滑ることで「気づき」があると信じていた。最近、世界的なフリースキーヤーに成長した佐々木悠は、日本に帰ってくると尾形さんの元にスキートレーニングに来ている。さらに、次の時代を担うフリースキーヤーとして期待を集めている佐々木玄も、次のステップに向かうために頼っているのが尾形さんなのだ。
昔、スキーが上手くなるには、インストラクターになることが手っ取り早い手段だった。三浦雄一郎さんが冒険スキーヤーとしてチャレンジしていた頃の影響は凄まじく、日本各地からやる気と根性の塊のような、生きの良い輩がテイネに集まってきていた。そして、様々なジャンルにおいて日本トップレベルのスキーヤーが在籍するスノー

ドルフィンの名は日本中に轟き、スキー界に多大なる影響を及ぼしてきた。しかし、スキーヤーとしてさらに上を目指す夢に溢れたメンバーが、スクールのスタッフとしてインストラクターを続けながら夢を叶えることは難しく、スノードルフィンの将来を担うと期待されたメンバーに限って、卒業していくようになっていった。なんとなく薄れつつあるように見えるドルフィニズムは、実は卒業したりテイネを離れた人によっても受け継がれている。三浦敬三さんの奥義を継承する尾形さんが、26歳の佐々木玄を指南している姿を見ながら、社会に失われがちな縦の繋がりの大切さを改めて感じていた。

斜面が一度緩やかになり、その間に呼吸を整える。斜度変化の先に、深川の広大な農地のパノラマが広がってきた。尾形さんは当然スピードを緩めることはなく、そのまま飛び込むように急斜面に滑り込んでいった。「うおおお！！」この斜面に滑り込む時は、いつも無意識で叫んでしまう。左右に視界を遮るものがない超大斜面。ここまで開放感があり、標高差もある圧雪斜面はそうそう巡り合えるものではない。道北ならではのドライで引き締まった美しいコーデュロイに面白いようにエッジが食いつく。俺は、ジェットコースターのようなGを全身に感じながら、ターンを繰り返していった。一方、尾形さんの滑りを見ると、Gを上手く逃すようなターンを軽快な切り返しでつないでいた。尾形さんと同じような滑りを試みるのだが、力を抜くと

At Kamui Ski-links first thing in the morning, he welcomed me on a perfectly maintained course. There is no large accommodation facility at the foot of the snow resort, so it feels more like a small resort loved by locals, but in fact, its attractive slopes are second to none.
"Let's first go to the 'Gold course'," Mr. Ogata murmured, and he started to ski relaxed.
I chased him. He was going fast, so I would be separated if I was not careful. I could not believe that he was already sixty-three years old. I shifted my gear and tried to stay behind Mr. Ogata.
He is so cool.
A relaxed style only made possible by his perfect position. Such simplified and sophisticated movement, with only what is needed.
Skiing with him, I remembered Keizo Miura, who passed away fifteen years ago. Keizo-sensei (an honorific to show respect) was the father of Yuichiro Miura and a pioneer in the Japanese skiing society. He was a well-known legend who kept skiing until he was one hundred years old. Master Keizo was a real ski hermit. I heard that when you surpass the age of ninety, you may feel an overwhelming speed of aging that cannot be contested. What was done yesterday can no longer be done today. His passion for skiing never diminished at all despite all the difficulties he faced. He studied the tune-up of ski equipment, the theory of skiing, and kept standing on the snow. In his later years, it took a long time to prepare for skiing, and when he finally made it onto the snow, stock was used like a wand to make him stand

still. But once he put on his skis, it was as if he suddenly became decades younger, and he began to ski dynamically.
The ultimate energy-saving skiing technique, described as "skiing on bones," is a masterpiece. I felt like I had witnessed it, and I wanted to know the depth of skiing. Like an old man who was master of Kenpo defeating a big man with a single finger in the movie. Perhaps Master Keizo was a ski hermit who had reached a similar mystery.
There are countless ski apprentices of Master Keizo all over Japan and even the world. But I think Mr. Ogata is the one who inherits the most essence. I know I have learned many lessons skiing at Mr. Ogata's back.

Fukagawa's vast agricultural landscape spread in front of me beyond the change in slope. Mr. Ogata did not slow down at all, then skied into the steep slope as if he were jumping in.
"Wowww!"
I cannot hold my voice in whenever I jump into this slope. A super-large slope with no obstruction to the left or right. There are no other slopes like this, so open, with a big altitude difference, and packed in an ideal way. But it was rare to enjoy it in this super-good condition. The snow was dry, as expected in the northern Hokkaido area. When I glided, my edge of the ski easily curved through the beautiful corduroy pattern that the piste machine had created on the slope. I was making my turns, feeling gravity like a roller coaster all over my body. Looking at Mr. Ogata's skiing, his turns were

connected smoothly, without the influence of strong gravity. I tried to do the same, but when I loosened my body and relax, I could not do it. It was not a technique that I could acquire overnight.
"It is good to be young. If I lean like you do, I will break my bones. Hahaha."
Mr. Ogata laughed, and I laughed.
When I first met Mr. Ogata, he was thirty-seven years old. Now I am forty-seven years old, so technically I am not young at all. In his mind, I might be still nineteen years old, like when we first met. Several decades had passed between us.
Communication is important for skiers, and we can communicate something by skiing together. What we share when we ski together: the same slopes, the same scenery, and the same smile.
"Let's ski together."
There is a lot of content in these simple words.
Kamui has Mr. Ogata; if I want to ski with him, all I need is visit Kamui.
We drove to Furano on Route 38 with satisfaction. The sun was about to fall below the horizon, and we were colored in red by the setting sun.

どうしてもボロが出る。なるほど、一朝一夕で身に付く滑りではないということか。

「若いっていいね〜。俺がそんなにスネ傾けて滑ったら、骨折しちまうよ（笑）」

尾形さんは笑い、俺も笑った。俺が初めて尾形さんに出会った時、尾形さんの年齢は37歳。今の俺は47歳なので全く若くないのだが（笑）、お互いに重ねてきた歳月を想っていた。

スキーヤーにとって大切なコミュニケーション。一緒に滑ることでわかることがある。そこでシェアした1本。シェアした景色、シェアした笑顔。「とりあえず一緒に滑ろう」この言葉は、実に奥が深いのだ。

そして、今日もまた自然体で滑り続ける。カムイには尾形さんがいる。なんともいえない安心感に包まれながら、俺たちは西日が差し込んだ38号線を富良野方面に車を走らせた。

Makoto Ogata

極寒の夜遊び 富良野、占冠中央、南富良野

最近、富良野を通りかかれば、必ずと言っていいほど訪れる場所がある。石黒孝幸さんが営むBARISTART COFFEEだ。もともと、石黒さんとは、お酒が大好きなスキーのお客さんが集まるツアーで知り合った。スキーバブルだった時期にデモンストレーターだった石黒さんは、飲み方も盛り上げ方も豪快で、ゴージャスな都会派スキーヤーという印象だった。そんな石黒さんが、大阪にある大企業を退職して、地元富良野に帰ってきたのは、富良野が外国人観光客に人気が出てきていたことにビッグチャンスを見出していたからだ。ところが、最悪のタイミングでコロナ禍に巻き込まれ、ライフプランがすっかり狂ってしまった。しかし、幸いだったのはスキーが大好きだったこと。何しろ、富良野という町はワールドクラスのスキー場が町民スキー場的な距離にあり、十勝連峰や夕張山地というバックカントリーエリアの宝庫も近くにあるスキーのパラダイスのような町なのだ。俺の地元の札幌でも、スキーをしない人はもったいないと思うけれど、富良野でスキーをやらないことは、例えるなら1億円のタンス貯金に一切手を付けずに貧乏暮らししているお婆ちゃんのようなものだ。俺が知っている石黒さんは、二日酔いで朝一のリフトに起きてこれない人だったけど、今は、早朝のパウダースノーを求める完全なローカルスキーヤーに変貌していた。スキーを縦に踏み込み、

ひらりひらりと舞うようにターンしてくる姿は、尾形さんと重なる部分もあるけれど、それとはまた一味違った華やかさがある。目立ちたがり屋のスターが多かったスキーバブル世代の中で、異彩を放ってきたキャラクターとスキー技術は流石の一言に尽きる。「いや〜俺なんて…」と謙遜しながらも、圭くんがカメラを構えると、本気で作品を残す滑りをしてくるのだ(笑)。この日の富良野スキー場は、滑っても滑っても斜面がリセットするほどの大雪で、二人とも全身雪にまみれて遊び続けた。
「タケちゃん、占冠中央スキー場って、行ったことある?」
北の峰ゴンドラに揺られながら、石黒さんは悪戯っぽい笑顔を浮かべて言った。そういえば、富良野近辺のナイタースキーのことで、石黒さんに相談していたのだ。
「…う〜ん、何となく存在は聞いていますけど、行ったことはないですね」
「リフト券が無料でさ、結構良い斜面なんだよ」
俺は、頭の中が大きなクエスチョンマークで満たされたが、気になって気になって仕方がなくなってしまった。

降りしきる雪は富良野の町を覆い尽くし、至る所で自家用車が雪にはまり動けなくなっている。富良野の町中でここまで積もることも珍

しい。俺はエンジンをふかして、除雪の追いつかないぬかるんだ国道に車を走らせていった。辿りつけるか心配な天気だったけど、38号線から分岐を占冠方面に向かい始める頃から降雪が止み、穏やかな空模様になってきた。「占冠にスキー場なんてあったかな〜?」と思いながら占冠に入ると、目の前にスキー場が現れた。
「めっちゃ目立つじゃん!(笑)」
トマムに向かう時にこの街を通過していたのは、かなり昔の事だが、当時の俺は、狭い斜面よりも広い斜面、低い山より高い山、緩い斜面より急な斜面、遅いリフトより早いリフト…という、若者にありがちな貧乏性な価値観の持ち主だったので、この素敵なスキー場が目に入らなかったようだ。占冠中央スキー場に着くと、2台の車がちょうど帰るところだった。夜の帳が下り始めた静かなスキー場にはほんのりとナイター照明が灯っていた。待ってましたと言うように休憩所の小屋から出てきたのが、石黒さんが紹介してくれた佐藤浩章さんだった。
「良い雪積もったんだけど、子供たちが滑ってギタギタにしちゃったんだよねー」
申し訳なさそうに言っているけど、斜面はキッチリと整備され、その上に5cmほどの粉雪。シュプールはたった4本しかついていないではないか。

Freezing night out Furano, Central-Shimukappu, South-Furano

When I have a chance to drive closer to Furano, there are places I want to visit.
One is Baristart Coffee, run by Takayuki Ishiguro. I first met him on a tour for customers, who ski and who loved drinking. Mr. Ishiguro was a demonstrator during the ski bubble, the way he drank together with ski fans was full of excitement and dynamic, and I had an impression of him as a gorgeous urban skier.
Mr. Ishiguro retired from a large company in Osaka and returned to his hometown, Furano, because he found that Furano had become popular with foreign tourists, making it attractive to set up shop there. However, it turned out to be the worst timing with this corona pandemic, and his life plan went completely crazy. A bad thing happened, but the good thing was, he loves skiing. And Furano is like a ski paradise, with world-class ski resorts and many attractive backcountry ski areas such as the Tokachi mountain range and the Yubari mountains nearby.
The man I had known was a person who had a hangover and didn't get up to ride the first lift in the morning back then. He had now completely transformed into a local skier seeking powder snow early in the morning.
Stepping on the skis vertically and turning like fluttering, some parts of his technique overlapped with Mr. Ogata's, and there were some different kinds of gorgeousness in Mr. Ishiguro's skiing.

"I'm just a small thing…" he said humbly. But his character and skiing technique were outstanding in the ski bubble generation. When Key held his camera, I was amazed by how he skied to fit into Key's perfect picture.

The snow at Furano Snow Resort on that day was so heavy that the slopes were recovered and reset easily; we enjoyed ourselves and had fun. Both of us continued to play in the snow and got covered in snow all over.

"Have you ever been to Shimukappu Chuou Ski Resort, Take-chan?" Mr. Ishiguro said to me with a mischievous smile when we were on the Kitanomine gondola. I had forgotten about it, but I was consulting with him about night skiing near Furano.
My reply was, "I've heard about it but never been there…"
My head was filled with big question marks, and I couldn't stop thinking about this Shimukappu Chuou Ski Resort.

With tips given by Mr. Ishiguro, we decided to head to Shimukappu. The falling heavy snow covered the city of Furano, and cars were starting to get stuck on the road everywhere. I ran the engine hard and drove down the road where the snow clearing service couldn't keep up. I was worried about the weather—whether we could reach Shimukappu or not due to this heavy

snow—but after we passed the junction of Route 38 and headed to Shimukappu, the snowfall had stopped, and we started to have clear skies.
On my way, I had no idea about the snow resort there at Shimukappu. But when I reached Shimukappu, there was a ski slope in front of me.
"Insanely noticeable!"
The last time I had passed this town was on my way to Tomamu, and it was a long, long time ago.
At that time, I was a person who only valued cost performance, which may tend to have this way of thinking when you are young, seeking a wider slope rather than a narrow one, a steeper slope rather than a gentle one. Therefore, I didn't recognize these nice ski slopes.

When we arrived at Shimukappu Chuou ski resort, two vehicles were about to leave. The slopes were lightening up softly a few hours after sunset.
It was Mr. Sato, who was introduced by Mr. Ishiguro, who came out of the rest area as if he was waiting for us.
"Sorry to inform you that we had some fresh snow, but kids ate [enjoyed] it all."
Mr. Sato apologized, but the slopes were well maintained, and there was about five centimeters of fresh powder on them. There were only four spurs; for me, this is nothing.

「ぜんぜんギタギタじゃないです！ むしろ最高です！(笑)」
早速滑る準備を済ませてロープトー乗り場に行くと、ロープトーは止まっていた。いや、係のおじさんに挨拶して動かしてもらうスタイルなのだ。無料で滑る俺たちをおじさんたちが見守ってくれていることに、なんとも言えない温かさを感じる。ロープトーを降りると、もう一つ上のロープトーに同じ要領で乗車する。温かい缶コーヒーくらい差し入れしたい気持ちになった。山頂と言うには低い丘の上から、占冠の灯りが少ない夜景を見下ろしながら、子供たちが歩いて通える場所にこのようなスキー場がある価値をしみじみ思っていた。他所から人がほとんど訪れない厳冬期の村に毎晩ナイタースキーの照明が灯り、寒さを忘れて滑る子供たちの笑い声が響く。このスキー場ができた時、地元の人々は厳しすぎる冬を照らす光を見たと思うのだ。「このようなスキー場がずっと続いていきますように」いろいろな思いを乗せながら、スキーは徐々にスピードを上げていく。中腹のL字カーブで失わないように軸を傾けて進入していくと、カーブの先に夜景が見えてきた。ここから斜度が少し増し、その先が横幅の広いメインの斜面だ。
劇場のスポットライトのように照らされている場所を目がけてスピードを上げ、ダンスをするかのようにターンを決めていく。滑り切ると静かな空気が戻ってきた。滑っているときと、止まったときと、違う空気を感じるのはスキーの面白いところだ。同行していた佐藤さんは、突如訪れた珍客の姿を目を細めて眺めていた。

この滑走で火がついた俺たちは、富良野に帰る途中にある南富良野スキー場に立ち寄った。低気圧の通過により吹雪が続いていたけれど、その後、風向きが変わるにつれて、みるみる気温が下がっていった。キュッキュと雪鳴りする足元を踏みしめてスキーセンターに行くと、地元のレーシングチームの子供たちや、アルペンスノーボーダーで思ったよりも賑わっていた。
「がはは！ さ、さみーーー！」
超低速のペアリフトの上で凍えながら、思わず笑ってしまった。ここ数年、日本は暖冬の影響で小雪に悩まされ、特に西日本での雪不足は深刻だった。どれだけのスキーヤーがお天道さまに寒気の到来を祈っただろうか。身体はガタガタ震え、鼻で息を吸うとツンと突き上げるようだ。手は悴み、バラクラバとゴーグルとの僅かな隙間が刺すように冷たい。
「俺たちは幸せだ」
寒さと言う名の恵みを全身で抱きしめたかった。バッチリ雪が締まった異様に広い上級者コースには、ほとんどスキーの跡がついていなかった。コースの広さに対して少ないナイター照明が、ポツンポツンと光の灯った島を出現させている。俺は闇と光を交互に浴びながら、スキーのエッジを雪面に食い込ませた。
俺は、アプレスキー（アフタースキー）もスキーの一部だと思っているタイプだ。早朝から夕方までしっかり遊び、温泉や食事やお酒を存分に楽しむ。だから、ナイタースキーを滑るのは年間数回が良いところ。だけど滑るたびに「やっぱり良いな」と思うのだ。寒さを抱きしめ、光と踊るスキー。景色が闇に消されると、視覚以外の感覚が鋭くなる。エッジが雪を切る音や風の音、夜の静けさ…。肌を叩く風の感触と冷たさ…。
駐車場までの緩斜面にスキーを滑らせながら、自然と言葉が口を突いて出てきた。
「来年はもっとナイターに来よう」

"It is not damaged at all! This is great (for us)!"
After we prepared in a hurry, we noticed the rope-tow platform had stopped. And we needed to ask for assistance from the person in charge to move the rope-tow for us.
When I got off the first rope-tow, there was another rope-tow, so I asked and got on it in the same way. With the operators' kind warm greetings, I wanted to hand a warm canned coffee to them for waiting for us to get these rope-tows ready.
When I reached the peak or, better to say, the top of the hill, looking down at Shimukappu's few bright lights, I thought about the value of ski slopes like this which children can visit on foot and enjoy when they want. The night lights of the slopes are lit every night in the village in the mid-winter, assuming they are rarely visited by people from other places. Kids playing forget about the cold with big smiles, and their laughter will echo in the slopes. When this ski resort was built, it was a big hope and savior in this harsh winter climate.
"May this kind of ski resort continue forever."
I skied with all the inputs and increased my speed.
With the cold weather in Shimukappu, there was a hard base of snow on the slopes. The surface was covered with dry snowflakes, which had been crushed in the sky and piled up evenly and smoothly. I increased my speed on a gentle slope in the beginning and tried not to slow down at the L-shaped curve on the hillside; then I faced the main wide slope, where Key could see me like a spotlight in the theater. I made turns like I was dancing. When I reached the bottom, I felt the calm energy of this hill. I feel deference when I am skiing on the slopes, and when I stand on them. This deference is the interesting part of the snow slopes. Mr. Sato accompanied us all the way, a bit surprised but also smiling.

We were motivated by this run and stopped by the Minimifurano Ski Resort on our way home.
As the low pressure passed and the wind changed direction, the temperature dropped. The snow squeaked when you stepped on it. When I reached the ski center, it was more crowded than I expected, full of children of the local racing team and families.
"Bahaha! Too freezing."
I laughed unintentionally while freezing on a low-speed pair lift.
Over the last few years, Japan has been cursed by very few snows due to the effects of mild winters, especially in western side of Japan. I am sure that many skiers prayed to the Snow Queen, begging for snow and chills.
My body start to shiver, and when I breathed in, my nose's chilliness hurt, my hands crushed. My face exposed between goggles and balaclava was pierced by the cold.
"Oh, it feels good to be loved by the Snow Queen."
We had been hungry to feel this coldness last winter; now I was filled with coldness and feeling damn good.
The wide black diamond slope was empty, and there were a few tracks curved on a well-packed slope. Only parts of the course were lit, making the slope into islands of light in the darkness. I skied through the darkness and light and curved my edge into the snow.
I have always thought that après-ski (French; in English, after-ski) is a part of skiing activities. Play hard from early morning to evening, then enjoy hot springs and good food with sake (drinks). For me, there may be only a few times to ski at night in one season. But when I have a chance to go night skiing, I always remember the good vibe, feeling the coldness and dancing with the light as I go down the slopes. When the scenery is erased by darkness, the senses other than vision become sharper. Sound of edges curving snow, winds and silence of the night… the feel of the wind that hits the skin and chilliness.
Skiing down the last gentle slope toward the parking lot, words naturally came out of my mouth:
"Let's go night skiing more next year."

Takayuki Ishiguro

DEEEEPな季節 旭岳

カムイミンタラ。
なんとなく神秘的な響きを持つこの単語は、北海道に住んでいるスキーヤー・スノーボーダーにとって特別な場所を指す。自然に畏敬の念を持ちながら、自然と共生してきたアイヌの人々は、大雪山のことをカムイミンタラ（神々の遊ぶ庭）と呼び、崇敬の対象としてきた。様々な信仰があるけれど、例えばチベット密教の場合、神聖なる山に登るのは禁忌とされることが多い。一方、自然の様々な現象や生き物、火や水、生活に必要な道具に神が宿っていると考えていたアイヌの人々にとっての山は、人々に開かれた「恵まれた場所」という意味あいが強いように思える。
世界中の雪山を旅してきた俺だが、大雪山（カムイミンタラ）に対する憧れは、いまだに変わらない。いや、それどころか高まるばかりだ。北海道好きの戯言と思われるかもしれないけれど、北海道そのものが奇跡だと俺は本気で信じているのだ（うざいって？笑）。まず、その特徴的な北海道の輪郭。こんなに個性があって形自体がロゴになり得る島って、他にそうそうあるものではない。そして、ちょうど良い緯度と立地。俺から言うと、神様が雪の天国として北海道を作ったとしか思えないのだ。世界で最も寒い地域の一つである極東シベリアは雪を降らせるために必要な寒気を育てる巨大な工場だ。この寒気

（シベリア高気圧）が発達して西高東低の気圧配置になると、北海道方面に超絶冷たい空気が流れ込む。この時、温暖な日本海にたまった湿気で雪雲を生成し、標高1,000m前後のちょうど良い高さの山々にどんどん雪を降らせるのだ。
幼少から札幌で育った俺は、海抜0mでもフワフワの粉雪という、世界でも稀有な条件を当たり前のことだと思っていた。戦後世代というほどの年齢ではないけれど、自信喪失した社会で育ったせいか？日本は狭く、日本は弱く、すごいものは全て外国にあると思っていた俺は、スキーで夢が広がると同時に、海外の山々に想いを馳せるようになった。海外に行って驚いたのは、山の大きさとスキーヤーの強さだ。子供の頃から厳しい急斜面で飛んだり跳ねたり直滑降したりして遊んできた選手たちと同じ斜面で滑りを競い合う中で、日本で滑るだけではスキーヤーとしてレベルアップが図れないことを悟った。同時に一つの疑問が浮かび上がってきた。俺が篭っていたコロラドのクレステッドビュートでは、まとまったパウダーが積もる事は滅多になく、数センチ積もっただけで崖からスキーヤーが次々と飛んでいた。木々の間もくまなくコブが発達し、斜面の至る所に岩が露出している。俺は、そんな厳ついスキー場で、パウダースノーのスプレーよりも、エッジが削れる火花を散らしながら滑ることの方が多かった。

やがて、大会や撮影で世界中を渡り歩くようになり、滑れば滑るほど気になっていたことが、ある確信へと変わっていくのだった。
「もしかして、北海道の雪が一番良いんじゃない？」
そう思いながら、地元北海道で滑る時は、雪質やリセット率（滑った斜面に雪が積もってリセットする頻度）に注意しながら滑ってみた。そこでまず驚いたのが、本当に高いリセット率だ。アメリカのコロラドは内陸にあるため、かなり勢力のあるストームが来なければ、なかなかまとまった雪が降ることはなかったが、日本の場合は北～西寄りの風が軽く吹くだけで至る所に雪雲が発生し、日本海側の山間部では毎日のように20～30cmの降雪があるのだ。これに気づいた俺は、嬉しすぎて昼食を食べる間も惜しんで滑りまくった。
当時は深雪滑走用のスキー（ファットスキー）もなく、外国人のスキーヤーもいなかったので、バックカントリーエリアは常に貸し切り状態だった。しかも、コロラドの標高が高いスキー場で篭っていた俺にとって、日本の雪山は標高が低く空気が濃厚で、気象条件も比較的穏やかだ。豪雪直後やホワイトアウトの時、北米のスキー場ではまともに滑れない条件になってしまうこともあったけど、日本のBCはツリーランなので、悪天候の時も滑ることができる。要するに、雪山に行けばほぼ100％パウダーにありつけるという信じられない世界だった。

DEEEEP season Asahidake

"Kamui Mintara"
This word, which has a somewhat mysterious sound, refers to a special place for skiers and snowboarders living in Hokkaido.

The Ainu people, who have lived in harmony with nature while being in awe of nature, call Daisetsuzan "Kamui Mintara" (the garden where the gods play) in the Ainu language, and it has been an object of reverence.
There are various beliefs. First, for example in the case of Tibetan Buddhism, climbing a sacred mountain is often contraindicated. On the other hand, for the Ainu people who thought that God dwelt in various phenomena and creatures of nature, fire and water, and tools necessary for life, the mountain means "a blessed place" that support people's living.
I have traveled to snowy mountains all over the world, but my aspiration for Daisetsuzan (Kamui Mintara) is still the same; no, it might just have grown over the years.
I really believe Hokkaido itself is a miracle. First, shape of the Hokkaido island is catchy and unique, so you will memorize it instantly. There is no other island like Hokkaido. Second, it has just the right latitude and location, selected by God to become a paradise of snow. Far East Siberia, one of the coldest regions in the world, is a huge factory that grows the cold air needed to make it snow.

When this cold Siberian air develops and the pressure distribution is high in the west and low in the east, super-cold air flows in Hokkaido's direction. At the same time, snow clouds are created by the humidity accumulated over the warm Sea of Japan and make it snow more and more on mountains at an altitude of around one thousand meters.
I grew up in Sapporo, so for me, fluffy powder snow at sea level was usual, though it is rare in the world. I am not so old as the post-war generation, but I am Generation X. Since I grew up in a society that lacked confidence—Japan is small, weak, and nothing to be proud of—I believed that all the great things existed overseas. When my dreams of skiing spread, I began to think about the foreign mountains. What surprised me when I went abroad was the size of the mountains and physical strength of the skiers.
I found that it would be necessary to ski abroad to improve my level as a skier, as I was competing with athletes who had been playing on steep slopes since childhood. At the same time, one question came up. Colorado's Crested Butte, which I picked as a place of training, was rarely covered with powder snow. When it was rarely blessed by just one inch of powder snow (1 inch = 2.54 cm), I saw many freaks jumping off the cliff. Bumps had also developed between the trees and crags exposed in the slopes; at such a harsh ski resort, I used to ski more often with sparks from the rocks sharpening my edges than with spraying powder snow. Then I began to

travel around the world at competitions and filming. The more I skied, the more I started to think about this, which turned into a certain conviction.
"Maybe the snow in Hokkaido is the best?"
After I noticed how much we are blessed, I tried to pay more attention to the quality of the snow and the reset rate (the frequency with which snow accumulates on the slopes and resets as a decent amount of fresh powder snow to enjoy). The first thing that surprised me was the really high reset rate
Since Colorado in the United States is inland, they need to have a substantially powerful storm to have enough snow to enjoy. For us, we only need a light wind from the north to the west that generates snow clouds, and in the mountains on the Sea of Japan side, there is snowfall of twenty to thirty centimeters on a daily basis.
When I noticed this, I was so happy that I skied without stopping to eat lunch. At that time, there were no skiers with fat skis and no foreign skiers, so the backcountry fields were always preserved and reserved for me.
Since the altitude of snowy mountains in Japan is much lower than in Colorado, the air in the Japanese mountains is rich, and the weather conditions are relatively mild. After the heavy snowfall or whiteout during the storm, in North America, snow resort conditions become too tough, and you may stay inside. In Japan, we can still enjoy the tree run when we have

その頃、美瑛に住む冒険野郎仲間の餌取浩さん（※）宅にみんなで居候しながら、大雪山を滑る日々が始まった。テイネやニセコではたっぷり滑ってきたけれど、大雪山を滑るのは3年前に旭岳で開催されたエクストリームスキーの日本一決定戦に参戦した時以来だ。あの時は、濃霧で競技者全員がノロノロ滑走していたのに、最終出走者の自分のスタート時に突如快晴となった。勝利を確信した若かりし（バカかりし）俺は、直滑降で樹林帯につっこんで大怪我を負ったのだ。旭岳は人生で最もかっこ悪い出来事があった因縁の山だった。あの時は直滑降しかしていないので斜面をよく覚えていないし、雪は暴風で叩きつけられたクラストだったので、正直言ってあまり期待しなかった。ロープウェイを降りて滑り出すと、すぐに異変に気がついた。

「何じゃこりゃ？」

太腿まで積もったディープパウダーだというのに、何の抵抗もなくスキーは進んでいく。例えるならば、羽毛をもっと軽くしたような…フワフワな泡のような…何とも言えない滑り心地だ。起きている現象に戸惑いながらも、その心地よさに酔いしれながらスキーを滑らせていく。途中から大きな斜度変化があるが、そのまま体の力を抜き、深海に身を委ねて沈んでいくダイバーのように、急斜面に滑り込んでいった。ニセコやテイネを滑っている時、スキーの滑走面で雪を掴み、サーフィンのように浮遊しながら雪を滑走していた。しかし、ここの雪はどうだろうか？雪の上を滑走しているのではなく、雪の結晶に満たされた空間を落下していく気分だ。頭の上まで埋まるような深さなのにスキーは軽く、左右上下、自由自在に動く。胸で押した雪の結晶が胸の前で小さな波をおこし、一緒に落下していく。巻き上がった雪の結晶は、再び雪面に戻ることはなく、凍てつき乾いた大気に昇華して、最後にキラキラと煌めいて消えた。滑り終えた俺は、信じられない気分で斜面を振り返った。

「…え？」

雪面のずっと下まで潜って滑ってきたというのに、ほとんどシュプールが残っていなかったのだ。注意深く見ると、ほんの少しだけ雪面が沈んでいるように見えた。なんとスキーヤーがかき分けた雪が、サラサラとシュプールに流れ込んで跡を消していたのだ。この時に感じた衝撃的で夢のような感覚は、25年経った今でも鮮明に覚えている。あの時の雪が、今のところ「人生で最も良い雪」になっているのだが、それに匹敵する雪をあと3回経験している。その1回が旭岳で、残り2回が富良野岳だった。

時は流れて、2021年の3月上旬。1台のRV車が雪煙を巻き上げながら、旭岳ロープウェイの駐車場に現れた。車から降りてきた初老の紳士が、神妙な面持ちでゆっくりと風景を眺めまわした。

「おはようございます！」

圭くんが紳士に声をかけると、彼は表情を崩し子供みたいな屈託ない笑顔を浮かべて言った。

「圭さんと滑る時は、必ず降って晴れますねぇ」

トランクからお気に入りのファットスキーを取り出しながら、落ち着いて準備をしているように見えてワクワクを隠せない様子が伝わってきた。スキー業界や観光業界で、彼のことを知らない人はいないだろう。様々な観光事業やスキー事業を成功させ、それぞれの業界で再生請負人と呼ばれている星野佳路さんだ。

コロナ禍という大変な状況の中、一貫したプラス思考で強気の発言は話題を呼び、今や、彼の一挙一動に社会全体が注目している。星野さんの経営者としての手腕はもちろん尊敬に値する部分だが、俺はそれ以上に、一人のスキーヤーとしての側面に興味が湧いていた。分単位でスケジュールがあるような超多忙な社長にして、年間滑走日数60日は尋常ではない。

（※）餌取浩さん、美瑛在住のレジェンドテレマークスキーヤー。現在は地元でガイドやゲストハウスを営む。

---

difficult conditions.
In short, Japan is the dreamland where you can get almost 100 percent powder snow when you head to the snowy mountains.

Around that time, while staying at the house of Etori-san（※）, who lives in Biei, the days of skiing on Daisetsuzan began for me. I've skied a lot in Teine and Niseko, but I haven't skied in Daisetsuzan since I participated in the National Extreme Skiing competition held at Asahidake three years ago. The weather was bad, and all the athletes were skiing slowly through the thick fog, but at the time the final runner, which was me, was about to start, suddenly it became fine and clear. At the start, as a young man who was convinced of victory, I skied straight down into the forest belt and got injured. Asahidake (one of the mountains in the Daisetsuzan mountain range) was the mountain where I had one of the worst events in my life. I didn't really expect much from this mountain because I didn't remember the slopes well at that time, since I had only skied straight down and crashed into the woods; the snow had been a crust due to the storm.
As soon as I got off the ropeway and started to ski, I noticed it was completely different from my expectation.
"What the heck??"
Even though it was a deep powder above my thighs, my skis just slid without any resistance.
For example, it's like light feathers, like a fluffy foam… It's an indescribable feeling. While being puzzled by the phenomenon that was happening, I was enjoying how my skis floated in the snow. After a while, a big slope steepness change approached, and I relaxed and dived into the steep slope like a diver into the ocean.
While skiing in Niseko or Teine, I would ski on the snow like I was surfing, catching snow with my skis. But at Asahidake at that time, I was gliding down a space filled with fluffy snow, literally skiing in the snow. It was deep enough to cover the top of my head, and my skis were free to move exactly I wanted from side to side and up and down. The snowflakes pushed by my chest made small waves in front me and fell together. When I finished skiing down, I looked back at my traces with disbelief.
"What?"
Even though I had skied all the way down the snow surface, there was almost no track left behind. When I looked carefully, it seemed that the snow surface had sunk a little. The snow that the skiers had squeezed out flowed into the track, erasing the traces. I still vividly remember the shocking and dreamy feeling I felt at that time, even after twenty-five years. The snow at that time was the best snow in my life so far. I have experienced three more occasions comparable to it. One was Asahidake the other day, and the other two were at Mt. Furano.

Time has passed, early March 2021.
A sports utility vehicle appeared in the parking lot of Asahidake Ropeway, rolling up snow and smoke. An elderly gentleman got out of the car slowly and looked mysteriously around the landscape.
"Good morning, sir!" Key called out to the gentleman, smiling like a child without any worry.
"When I ski with you, Key-san, it always snows and then gets sunny."
As he took out his favorite fat skis from his vehicle's trunk, I could see that he couldn't hold in his excitement while he pretended to prepare calmly.
Everyone in the ski or tourism industry knows Yoshiharu Hoshino, who has succeeded in various tourism and skiing businesses and is called the "Last Chance" in each industry. In the situation of the declining ski population and the corona pandemic, his positive mindset and confident remarks are taken highly, and his every move is the center of attention. Mr. Hoshino's skill as an executive is of course worthy of respect, but I was interested more in the aspect of a skier who loved skiing more than me. For a super-busy president who has a schedule in minutes, sixty days dedicated to skiing in a year is unusual.

（※）Etori-san、The Legend telemark skier. He manages a guide and a guest house.

旭岳の山頂から山麓の駅舎まで、満遍なく上質の羽雪が30cmほど降り積もっていた。標高が高い旭岳で、全標高全方位に満遍なく雪がつくことは相当珍しいことだ。そして、非の打ちどころのないブルースカイとキリッと澄んだ大気が、夕刻まで完璧に晴れ続けることを約束してくれているように思えた。こんな天気に出会った時、今まで稜線で震えた時の辛さがキレイさっぱり吹っ飛んで消えていくのだ。ただ単に雪の上を風のように一気に滑り降りるだけの、この遊び。そんな時間を何よりも大切にしている星野さんと共感し合えることを俺は心から嬉しく思った。1日が24時間なのは誰にでも変わらないけれど、その密度には個人差があると思う。有限な時間をどのように使うのか。自分自身にとって何が大切なのかを星野さんは完全に理解されていて、何事にも清々しいくらい凛とした自分の姿勢を持っているのだ。
「最近は、スキーをするために仕事を決めるようになりましたね。スキー中心主義ですね。あとは、私は花粉症なので、花粉の多い時期は本州にいないようにしています。その延長で、今度は雪が降った時は仕事しないとか、天気中心主義で働きたいと思ってますよ（笑）」
不思議な方だ。きっと口にすることのほとんどをやってのけてしまうのに違いない。星野さんと一緒にいると、自分にとって大切なことのために時間を使わなければ損だ！という気持ちになる。同じ斜面を共有し、時間を共有し、感動を共有する。スキーセッションというのは、

本当に素晴らしい。プロスキーヤーと経営者という全く違う立場の二人が、たった数本をシェアしただけで、旧知の友のように分かり合えた気がするのだ。数本滑って満足感を得られたので、ロープウェイ駅舎にある食堂で昼食を取ることにした。そこで星野さんは何の迷いもなくカツカレーを注文した。
「私は、日本中のスキー場でカツカレーを食べようと思っているんですよ（笑）」
この人は本当に楽しみ方を知っている人だ。また雪上で会う日は、またそう遠くない未来に、自然と訪れることだろう。きっと星野さんも同じことを思っていたに違いない。

「今日はピンクになりそうだね」
圭くんが空を見上げながら言った。日中で美味しいところを十分に滑った星野さんは、区切りの良いところで切り上げて仕事に戻っていった。一方、圭くんと俺は、日没までじっくり滑る意気込みでいた。滑る分には午前中が最高だけれど、撮影には昼下がりから日没までの時間が魅力的なのだ。午後の少し黄色味がかった西日は、徐々に黄金色に変わり、赤い絵具を少しずつ溶かすように雪を染めていく。赤みが濃くなるにつれて影の青みが増していき、山の地形や雪の質感を浮き彫りにしていく。ここまではよくある快晴で、本番はこれからだ。

太陽が地平線に差し掛かると、明るさは少しトーンダウンしながら山全体をピンク色に染め、日陰部分は紫色に変化する。一番きれいなピンク色はほんの2〜3分。わずか数分間のスペクタクル。雪山でなければ見られない色彩の魔法。雪は白いと思っている人が多いけれど、それはあまりにも浅はかだ。雪の色ほど変化する物はこの世に存在しないと思うのだ。スキー写真を何十年と追いかけてきているけれど、どの写真をとっても雪の質感や色合いは違う。山から人の姿は消え、ピンク色に染まった斜面は、いつもより静かな佇まいをしているように見えた。一日中天気だったというのに西日が当たるこの斜面が粉雪で残っていることは、厳冬期ならではの恵みだ。俺は、雪の感触と網膜に反射する色彩を噛み締めるようにターンを刻んでいった。
「最高だなぁ…」
一通りの撮影を終えた圭くんは、なおも色合いを変えていく山並みと空の美しさに浸っている。本当は、いつまでもここに留まっていたいのだろう。圭くんの満たされた表情を見ながら、やっぱりこの人は写真家になるために生まれてきたような人だと、俺は思っていた。

From the summit of Asahidake to the station building at the foot of the mountain, about thirty centimeters of high-quality featherlight snow was piled up evenly. At high altitude like Asahidake, it is quite rare to be covered by snow evenly in all directions, since the influence of the wind is strong. The impeccable blue sky and crisp, clear atmosphere seemed to promise to stay perfectly sunny until evening. I was simply happy to be able to ski with Mr. Hoshino, who cherishes his time skiing like the wind above all else. Everyone has twenty-four hours a day, but I think there are individual differences in the density. How to spend a finite amount of time. I think that he has clear priorities, and he has a refreshingly dignified attitude in everything.
"Recently, I've decided to work for skiing. A 'ski-centric life.' I have hay fever, so I don't go to mainland Japan when it's allergy season. Also, I am trying to apply my rules with a broader interpretation, like when I'm blessed with snows, I do not work. I want to work on a 'weather-centric' basis," he said, laughing.
He is a man of his words. When I'm with him, I am always encouraged to seize the day.
Share the same slopes, share time, share emotions. The ski sessions are really great. It feels like two people, a professional skier and an executive, who are in completely different positions can understand each other like old friends by sharing only a few slopes together.
After a few slopes together, we were satisfied and decided to have lunch at the cafeteria in the ropeway station building.
Mr. Hoshino ordered curry with deep-fried pork without any hesitation.
"I'm thinking of eating curry with deep-fried pork at ski resorts all over Japan," he laughed.
He knows how to enjoy himself. He knows where to find the good snow; we may encounter each other and have chance to ski together in the near future. I'm sure Mr. Hoshino was thinking the same thing.
After he had enjoyed enough of the splendid snow, he rounded up his gear and returned to work.
On the other hand, Key and I were enthusiastic to continue our shooting until sunset. The morning is the best for skiing, but the time from early afternoon to sunset is attractive for shooting.
The sun in the afternoon, slightly yellowish from the west, gradually turns to gold and dyes the snow with red paint. As the red color gets darker, the blue color of the shadow increases.
The shape of the mountains and the texture of the snow will be highlighted.
It's been sunny so far, and there's more to come.
As the sun approaches the horizon, the brightness turns a little darker, dyeing the entire mountain pink and then purple.
The most beautiful pink color only lasts a few minutes. A spectacle for just a few minutes. The magic of color that can only be seen in snowy mountains. Many people think that the color of snow is white, but that's too shallow-minded.

I don't think there is anything in the world that changes as much as the color of snow.
Even though it was sunny all day long and this slope had been exposed to sun from the west, it was still preserving powder snow. This is the blessing of midwinter.
I was trying to memorize the touch of snow and the many colors that my eyes caught as I skied down the slope.
"Awesome…"
After finishing all the shooting, Key was still immersed in the beauty of the mountains, the sky still changing colors.
We could stay here forever. Looking at Key's fully satisfied expression, I thought he was born to be a photographer.

北海道 パウダーベルト の滑り方 how to ride the Hokkaido
by Takeshi Kodama , Key Sato

児玉　毅：プロスキーヤー　1974年7月28日生 札幌市出身
Takeshi Kodama : Professional skier　Born July 28, 1974 / Birthplace : Sapporo, Hokkaido

大学に入ってからスキーにハマった遅咲きのプロスキーヤー。
卒業後、スキー武者修行のため単身アメリカへ。その後、エクストリームスキーのワールドツアーに参戦しながら、国内外の難斜面、極地、高所、僻地などでスキー遠征を重ねる。2000年北米大陸最高峰デナリ山頂からスキー滑降、2003年シーカヤックを用いた

グリーンランドでのスキー遠征、2008年ヒマラヤ未踏峰での初滑降など、世界各地にシュプールを刻み、2005年には何故かエベレストにも登頂。
撮影活動も精力的に行っており、スノー系専門誌を中心に掲載多数、DVD作品23タイトル、TV番組「LOVE SKI HOKKAIDO」などにも出演。

A professional skier who became addicted to skiing during his college years. After graduation, he went to the USA alone for ski training. Then participated in both overseas and Japanese expeditions on difficult slopes in extreme regions, high places, and difficult-to-access areas while he competed in the Extreme Ski World Tour.

In 2000, he skied downhill from the summit of Denali, the highest peak on the North American continent. In 2003, he made a ski expedition in Greenland with sea kayaking. In 2008, he made the first downhill run in the Himalayas' unexplored peaks. Curving his spur around the world, he also climbed to Mt. Everest's peak in 2005.

佐藤　圭：フォトグラファー　1972年3月19日生 札幌市出身
Key Sato : Photographer　Born March 19, 1972 / Birthplace: Sapporo, Hokkaido

2009年に大雪山十勝岳エリアの懐、上富良野町に移住し、そこを拠点にスキー・スノーボードの撮影をメイン活動。メーカーカタログ、雑誌等で多数発表。世界各地を訪れ、国内外問わず様々な土地で、多くのライダーとのセッションをライフワークとする。スキーとスノーボードの写真をバランスよく撮影し、被写体となるライダーの数は業界No.1。また、今回、旅の拠点となったゲストハウス「オレンジハウス」を運営している。

In 2009, Key moved to Kami-Furano, the skirt of the Daisetsuzan Tokachidake. Based there, he mainly shoots ski and snowboard photography. His work is in many manufacturer catalogs and magazines, etc. His life's work is visiting all over the world, including Japan, and doing sessions with many riders. The numbers of riders is well balanced between skiers and snowboarders, and he shoots with the largest number of riders in the industry. He owns the "Orange House," which was the base of the trip.

北海道パウダーベルトとは　What is the Hokkaido Powder Belt?

北海道の中央に位置し、世界一と言っても過言ではないほど上質のパウダースノーを楽しめる旭岳、黒岳、カムイ、富良野、トマムなどのスキー場とその周辺のバックカントリーをまとめた総称。
豪雪のニセコエリアなどに比べ、降雪量はやや少ないものの、低温で乾燥した気候により、一度降った雪のクオリティが長くキープされるのが特長。また、トマムのようなリゾート型のスキーが楽しめるエリアもあれば、旭川市街に宿泊して様々なスキーエリアを滑る都市型のスキー可能。スキー場をハシゴして遊べるような魅力的なローカルスキー場も多数あり、スキーを楽しむ上で、理想的なエリアとも言える。

HPB
Hokkaido Powder Belt

Located in the center of Hokkaido, it is a general term that encompasses ski resorts such as Asahidake, Kurodake, Kamui, Furano, and Tomamu and the surrounding backcountry area where you can enjoy high-quality powder snow that it is not an exaggeration to say is the best in the world.
The amount of snowfall is slightly less than in the Niseko area, but the quality of the snow is maintained and preserved for a long time due to the low temperature and dry climate. Also, there are areas where you can enjoy resort-type skiing such as Tomamu, and you can also enjoy various ski areas if you stay in the Asahikawa city area.

A 富良野スキー場

コース数23、最長滑走距離4,000mを誇る北海道を代表するスキー場の一つ。十勝連峰を望みながら滑走できる絶好のロケーションと、初心者から最上級者まで満足できるバリエーション豊富なコースレイアウト。オススメは富良野エリアトップからボトムまでの超ロングな圧雪バーン。パウダースノーを求める人には、北の峰エリアのプレミアムゾーンがオススメ。本格的なフリーライドを楽しむことができる。

Furano Ski Resort

One of Hokkaido's leading ski resorts, with a longest run of 4,000 meters, Furano Ski Resort boasts 23 courses. It is a great location, where you can ski or snowboard while looking at the breathtakingly beautiful Tokachi mountain range. Furthermore, there is a wide variety of course layouts that will satisfy both beginners and top-class players. We recommend the ultra-long well-packed snow slope in the Furano Zone. For those who want powder snow, we recommend going to the premium area in the Kitanomine Zone. You can enjoy a full-fledged free ride there.

B トマムリゾート

もはや日本を代表するスノーリゾートと言って良いだろう。幼児からお年寄りまで、スキー初心者からエキスパートまで、全ての客層に応えるスキーコースと、充実したサービスやアクティビティが魅力。プロスキーヤーの自分でも「ファミリーでゆっくり過ごしたいな〜」と思わせてくれる夢の国。

Hoshino Resorts TOMAMU

This is truly one of the snow resorts that best represents Japan. From infants to the elderly, from beginners to experts, Hoshino Resorts TOMAMU boasts ski courses that cater to all customers, as well as a full range of enjoyable services and activities. Indeed, this place is a dreamland where a professional skier would love to spend time with his family.

C カムイスキーリンクス

リゾートではないのに、それに勝るとも劣らない規模と高いポテンシャルを誇るスキーコース。絶対滑るべきは、国内でも類を見ない全幅150mのワイドな「ゴールドコース」。パウダーを滑りたい人にオススメなのが、第5リフト側にある「ディープパウダー」と「フレッシュパウダー」コース。お手軽に上質のパウダーが楽しめる。

Kamui Ski Links

Although it is not a resort, as there is no attached accommodation facility, Kamui Ski Links's slopes boast both a scale and potential as good as any other snow resorts. You should definitely ski at the wide "Gold Course," which is unprecedented in Japan, with a width of 150 meters. For those who want to enjoy powder snow, the "Deep Powder" and "Fresh Powder" courses on the fifth lift side are recommended. There, you can easily enjoy high-quality powder snow.

D サホロリゾート

晴天率が高く気温が低い条件で、常に安定した滑走条件を提供してくれるスキー場。十勝平野を望みながらの、グルームバーンをロングクルージングは快感度抜群。

Sahoro Ski Resort

A ski resort that always provides stable skiing conditions with a high possibility of sunny weather and low temperatures, Sahoro Ski Resort is worth a visit. Long cruising on the well-groomed slope while overlooking the Tokachi Plain is outstandingly pleasant.

E 比布スキー場

大きなスキー場ではないけれど、旭川市街から近く、全体的にバランスが良いコースレイアウトで、上達志向のスキーヤー・スノーボーダーやファミリーに愛されているスキー場。安価で美味しいゲレ食をお腹いっぱい食べれて、ベースには温泉施設も待っている理想的な町営スキー場。

Pippu Ski Resort

Although not a large ski resort, it is close to Asahikawa and has a well-balanced course layout, which skiers, snowboarders, and families who want to improve their skills love. Indeed, Pippu Ski Resort is an ideal town-run ski resort where you can eat inexpensive, delicious food and have hot spring facilities at the base.

F サンタプレゼントパーク

旭川市民に愛され続けている、まさに都市型スキー場の代名詞。どちらかというと初中級者やファミリー向けで、レンタルやスキースクールも充実しているので、旭川にステイして、家族で気軽に遊びに行ってみるのも良い。ここの名物は何と言っても旭川の夜景に飛び込むように滑れるナイター。

Santa Present Park

Santa Present Park is a symbolic urban ski resort that has been loved by Asahikawa citizens for years. This ski resort is for beginners, intermediates, and families. There are plenty of rentals available and ski schools, so it may be good idea to stay in Asahikawa while visiting. The specialty here is a night ski, where you can ski with a fabulous nighttime view of Asahikawa.

G 旭岳ロープウェー

大雪山のシンボル、旭岳を正面に望む姿見まで上がれるロープウェー。コースとは言っても、安全に下山するために圧雪された通路のようなものなので、滑走を楽しむのはバックカントリーエリアということになる。旭岳を楽しむためには十分な滑走技術と、バックカントリーの装備が必要になる。

Daisetuzan Asahidake Ropeway

A ropeway you can climb up to see Mount Asahidake of Daisetuzan Mountains, Daisetuzan Asahidake Ropeway is an experience like no other. Even though it is a course, it is like a snow-packed walkway for safe descent, complete with a backcountry area where you can enjoy skiing and snowboarding. Sufficient skills and backcountry equipment are required to enjoy Asahidake.

H 黒岳スキー場

登山の拠点となっている施設を冬季はスキー場として営業している。積雪期が長いこのスキー場は、特にシーズン始めと春の残雪シーズンに多くの利用客で賑わう。北向きの斜面なので雪質が安定して良く、バックカントリーエリアとしても人気だ。

Daisetsuzan Sounkyo Kurodake Ropeway

This facility is the base for mountaineering and is open as a ski slope during the winter. This ski slope, which has a long snow season, attracts many visitors, especially at the beginning of the season and during the remaining snow season in the spring. The slope faces north, so the snow quality is stable, and it is also popular as a backcountry area.

I キャンモアスキービレッジ

旭川空港から車で15分という好立地にあるスキー場。コンパクトながらも、この地域特有の粉雪と、広々としたコースで、特に初中級者やファミリーにオススメのスキー場だ。ナイター設備も充実しているので、旭岳の帰りに寄ってみるのもオススメ。

CANMORE Ski Village

A ski resort in a good location, CANMORE Ski Village is only a 15-minute drive from Asahikawa Airport. Although it is compact, it is a ski resort that is especially recommended for beginners and intermediate skiers and families due to the powder snow peculiar to this area and the spacious course. The night ski facilities are also substantial, so it is recommended to stop by on the way back from Asahidake.

J 美瑛町民スキー場 Biei Chomin Ski Resort	O 南富良野スキー場 National Minami-Furano Ski Resort
K 日の出スキー場 Hinode Ski Resort	P 占冠中央スキー場 National Shimukappu Ski Resort
L 上川町営中山スキー場 Kamikawa-cho Choei Nakayama Ski Resort	Q 中富良野北星スキー場 Naka-Furano Hokusei Ski Resort
M 愛別ファミリースキー場 Aibetsu Family Ski Resort	R 伊ノ沢スキー場 Inosawa Ski Resort
N 当麻町営スキー場 Touma Choei Ski Resort	S 新得山スキー場 Shintokuyama Ski Resort

Backcountry Area

十勝岳温泉エリア

北海道で一番標高が高い温泉、十勝岳温泉、吹上温泉をベースとするバックカントリーエリア。ここをベースに富良野岳、三峰山、三段山、十勝岳などのアルパインを滑るのが一般的だ。なんと言っても雪質が素晴らしく眺望も良いので、バックカントリースキーヤーにはたまらないエリアだ。

Tokachidake Onsen Area

This is a backcountry area located on the highest altitude hot springs in Hokkaido: Tokachidake hot springs and Fukiage hot springs. At Tokachidake Onsen Area, skiing or snowboarding on alpine terrain such as Furanodake, Sanpozan, Sandanyama, and Tokachidake are common. The snow quality in this area is excellent, and the view is splendid. Indeed, it is an area that is irresistible for backcountry skiers and snowboarders.

夕張山地エリア

富良野スキー場を北端に南北60kmに渡って連なる山々。富良野西岳、御茶々岳、芦別岳など、バックカントリーとして魅力的な山が連なるが、山が奥深く、長時間のハイクアップが必要となるので、上級者向きのエリアと言える。

Yubari Mountains Area

Here, mountains stretch 60 kilometers north and south, with Furano Ski Resort at the north end. Furano Nishidake, Ochachadake, Ashibetsu, and other attractive mountains are located in the backcountry area, but because they are not so easy to access and require long hikes, it is an area suitable only for advanced backcountry skiers and snowboarders.

表大雪エリア

北海道最高峰旭岳をシンボルとする、最も有名な大雪山エリア。旭岳温泉や黒岳温泉など登山の基地から、ロープウェーやリフトで大雪山にアプローチすることができる。当たった時の雪のクオリティはまさに世界一と言っても良いレベル。しかし、強風でロープウェーが運休することも多い。

Omotetaisetsu Area

This is the most famous Daisetsuzan area, with the symbol of Asahidake, the highest peak in Hokkaido. You can approach Daisetsuzan by ropeway or lift from mountain climbing bases such as Asahidake Onsen and Kurodake Onsen. The quality of the snow on the perfect day is truly incomparable. However, strong winds often suspend ropeways, so plan accordingly.

裏大雪エリア

冬期は深い雪に閉ざされ、近づくことができないが、6月中旬頃に、銀泉台や大雪高原温泉への道路が開通すると、残雪を求めるスキーヤー・スノーボーダーで賑わう。

Urataisetsu Area

In winter, the deep snow closes Urataisetsu Area, and it cannot be approached. But when the road to Ginsendai and Daisetsu Kogen Onsen opens in mid-June, it is crowded with skiers and snowboarders seeking to experience the remaining snow.

フォトグラファー佐藤圭目線のお店紹介 Shop introduction by Key Sato, Photographer

●東川 Higashikawa

SALT
カッチくんセレクトのお洒落な商品がたくさん。
山で使えるものもかなりあるので要チェック。
ドリンクのテイクアウトもできるので旭岳帰りに是非。

here are many fashionable products selected by Katchi-kun. Check it out—there are many items that you can use in the mountains. You can also take out drinks. I recommend you stop by on your way back from Asahidake.

りしり Rishiri
地元の人や観光客、そして滑り手で、いつも賑わっている超人気店。北海道や、東川町・上川盆地でしか食べれない新鮮な素材を活かした心のこもった料理を、美味しいお酒で、確実にいきたい！って方はご予約を！

A very popular izakaya that is always crowded with locals, tourists, skiers and snowboarders.
Enjoy hearty dishes made with fresh ingredients that can only be served in Hokkaido with delicious sake. If you want to be sure, please make a reservation!

ノマド Nomad
山帰りにふらっと寄りたくなるカフェ。店主はスキーヤーで山にも詳しいので、美味しいご飯を食べながら、山の情報をここでゲットしましょう。不定期で販売されるオリジナルCD「mountain time」もおすすめ。お山までのドライブお供に。

A café that makes you want to stop by on your way home from the mountains. The owner is a skier and familiar with the mountains, so you can get information about the mountains here while enjoying delicious food.

Yamatune
靴下屋さんのヤマチューン？ヤマツネ？どっちでも良いみたいです（笑）。オールシーズンで使えるソックスは、こだわり抜いて作られたオンリーワンな商品。今使ってるものに満足していない人、満足でも気になってる人、是非使ってみて下さい。RIDE THE EARTHとのコラボソックスがこの秋発売予定！

Unique socks that can be used in all seasons are made with great care. If you are not satisfied with what you are using now, or even if you are satisfied, please try them anyway.
Collaboration socks with "Ride the Earth" will be released this fall!

hotel ディアバレー Hotel Deer Valley
旭岳温泉街の入口から少し中に入ったところにあるホテル。落ち着く空間、客室、そして料理。全てが良くて癒されます。ゆっくりとした時間を過ごしたい時は是非この宿へ。

A hotel located a little inside the entrance of Asahidake Onsen. Calm space, guest rooms, and great food; you will be healed and relaxed. If you want to spend some relaxing quality time, this is the inn you definitely go to.

フィールドアーステストセンター field earth testcenter
メイドイン大雪山／旭川ブランドのフィールドアース唯一のテストセンター。旭岳に向かう途中のレンガ作りの建物。店内はスケートボードのランプ、クライミングウォール、もちろんフィールドアースのスノーボード、スキーのレンタルが可能。BLANKデッキのシェイプもできる。

The test center for made in Daisetsuzan/Asahikawa brand "Field Earth." Inside the store, you can enjoy skateboard ramps and climbing walls. And you can rent "Field Earth" snowboards and skis. You can also shape the blank deck here.

トランジット東川 Transit Higashikawa
マニアックかつ間違いない商品構成で人気のアウトドアギアショップ。迷っているものがあれば店主に相談してください。買いたくなる、つい買っちゃう的確なアドバイスをしてくれますよ（笑）。朝早くからオープンしているので、僕みたいな忘れ物王に本当にありがたいんです。

A popular outdoor gear shop with the lineup of a maniac and great products without a doubt.
If you have any questions, please consult with the shop owner; he will give you accurate advice that makes you want to buy. Open early in the morning, so it's a good idea to stop by on your way to the mountains.

ベレゾン Wine Café Veraison
お洒落なお店が多い東川、こちらもお洒落で雰囲気がいいですガラス張りの清潔感溢れる店内。ランチで食べることができるハンバーグが美味しくてオススメです。夜もソムリエでもある店主が選ぶワインと食事が楽しめますよ！

Higashikawa has many fashionable stores; this one is also fashionable and has a nice atmosphere, glass-walled with lots of light and cleanliness. The hamburger steak that you can order at lunch is delicious and recommended. You can enjoy wine and meals selected by the owner, who is also a sommelier at night.

●旭川 Asahikawa

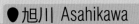

はたご Hatago
5・7小路ふらりーとの入口にある炉端焼きのお店。旬の食材や新鮮な海の幸を使った料理は何を食べても絶品。ぜひご予約をしてお出かけください。

Robatayaki restaurant at the entrance of Furarito (5jyo-doori 7choume). The dishes made with seasonal ingredients and fresh seafood are excellent no matter what you eat. Please make a reservation.

オモセブン omo7
市内の少し外れにある滑り手に大人気のホテル。1Fのラウンジの大スクリーンではいつも映像が流れ、夜な夜な滑り手たちで賑わっています。朝食のビュッフェも美味しくて、ついつい食べすぎちゃいます。サウナーには有名なサウナも人気です。近郊のスキー場情報も詳しく見れるのも嬉しいです。

A very popular hotel for skiers and snowboarders on the outskirts of the city. On the big screen of the lounge on the first floor, videos are always played, and it is crowded with skiers and snowboarders at night. The sauna here is also popular among sauna geeks. You can also check out detailed information on the snow resorts in nearby areas.

秀岳荘旭川 Shugakuso, Asahikawa branch
北海道のアウトドアショップといえば秀岳荘。その旭川店。人気の秘密は「ないものはない」というほど商品構成じゃないかな。何かあれば店員さんに聞けば絶対解決という間違いないショップ。僕もかなりわがまま言ってお世話になりっぱなしです。

Representative of an outdoor shop in Hokkaido. The secret of its popularity is the rich product lineup.
If there is something you need to solve, I think it will definitely be solved by asking the clerk.

ラーメン三日月 Ramen Mikazuki
地元や道内の滑り手から、密かに？結構？大分愛されている人気のラーメン店。いつも混んでいますが、待っても食べる価値アリな、ザ旭川ラーメン！

A popular ramen shop that is probably? Secretly? Very much? loved by the skiers and snowboarders, both locally and throughout Hokkaido. It's always crowded, but it's worth the wait! The Asahikawa ramen!

アサヒカワライド Asahikawa Ride
買い物公園に面した便利な立地にあるゲストハウス。夏は自転車好き、冬はスキー客で賑わい、看板猫ちゃんがお出迎えしてくれます。リーズナブルにステイしたい人にオススメ。

A guest house conveniently located facing the shopping park. Bicycle lovers in the summer, skiers and snowboarders in the winter, and the signboard cat welcome you. Recommended for those who want to stay reasonably.

パレンタ Palemta shop&gallery
北海道で採れた旬の野菜を中心にしたお食事を提供するカフェ。2Fにはショップ＆ギャラリー、隣にはデザインセンターがあり、旭川に触れることができる。

A café that serves meals of seasonal vegetables harvested in Hokkaido. The second floor is a shop and gallery, and you can touch Asahikawa's woodwork furniture at the design center next door.

フリーハウス ザ イースト Freehouse THE YEAST
買い物公園に面した絶好の立地で、食事の後にも気軽に寄れるクラフトビールの専門店。たくさんのクラフトビールがあり、中でもお店オリジナルのビールが最高！テイスティングセットもあるのでいろんなビールを試してみて下さい。

A craft beer specialty store that you can easily stop by after a meal in a great location facing the shopping park. There are many varieties of craft beers, and I think the shop's original beer is the best!

ジビエバル 山神 Jibie Bar YAMAGAMI
ジビエってけっこう敷居が高めなイメージだけど、このお店はリーズナブルでたくさんのメニューを提供してくれる。エゾ鹿、イノシシ、タイミングで熊！ほかにもいろいろ。鹿肉のレアカツはほんと美味い！

We have an image of expensive dishes for Jibie, but this restaurant is inexpensively priced and offers a lot of variety. Ezo deer, wild boar, and if you are lucky, you may enjoy bear! There are many others. The medium-rare fried venison cutlet is awesome!

● 富良野 Furano

バリスタート富良野
Baristart Coffee Furano

富良野の街中にある本格バリスタ。スキー帰りに美味しいコーヒーで一息。シーズン中は毎日朝イチ滑っている石黒さんとのスキー談義も楽しめます。

An authentic barista in the city of Furano. Take a break with delicious coffee on your way home from skiing. During the season, you can enjoy ski-talk with Mr. Ishiguro, who is skiing every morning.

ホルモン竹
Hormone TAKE

富良野ナイトの穴場！とにかく店主の竹さんが面白くて、ついつい長居してしまいます。ホルモンはもちろんお肉の種類も豊富で意外とリーズナブル。

A little-known spot in Furano at night! The owner, Take-san, is so funny that I just stay longer. Not only hormones (a kind of Korean BBQ common in Japan) but also many cuts of meats are available and inexpensive.

Furano bar

本格イタリアンでもてなしてくれるお店。ちょっと1杯、ゆっくり飲みたい、どんな時でも居心地が良いのでついゆっくりしてしまう。フードも通常メニューはもちろん絶品だけど、裏メニューもあるとかないとか？ワインの種類も豊富なので、料理に合う1杯を店長けんちゃんに聞いてみて下さい。

A restaurant that serves authentic Italian food. A quick drink, or a slow one—you can relax and feel at home either way, but usually I stay longer with the nice atmosphere. Of course, the food on the menu is excellent, but there is also a secret menu, I heard. There is a wide variety of wines, so ask the manager Ken-chan for a glass that goes well with the dish.

唯我独尊 Yuigadokuson

創業47年！ですって！
遠く九州の知り合いも富良野に来たら必ず行くという、全国にファンがいるカレー屋さん。カレーも手作りソーセージも燻製も作る人の思いを聞くとますますファンになりますね。毎回あの合言葉を言いたくて、ご飯大盛りでルーを先に食べきるのはお約束！ここも人気店でいつも混んでいますが、食べる価値おおありなので並んでも食べてみてー！

Founded 47 years ago, Yuigadokuson is a curry shop that has fans all over Japan. When I hear the stories of people who make curry, sausages, and smoked foods, I become more of a fan. It is always crowded here, but it is well worth it to wait in the line, so please try it!

緑輪堂 Enwado

僕は、ここのドーナツをしばらく食べてないと禁断症状が出ます（笑）。もっちもちのドーナツを山で食べるとシアワセになります。テイクアウト以外にも店内でイートインもできるので、お時間ある方は店内でゆっくりもありです。

I have withdrawal symptoms if I don't eat the donuts here for a while. This chewy donut makes me happy in the mountains. You can both eat in and take out.

カレーのふらのや
Curry FURANOYA

こちらも富良野スキー場帰りにマストな人気店。スープもルーもどちらも美味しいので、いつも迷っちゃうんですよね。僕は野菜スープカレー3番ナス抜き（笑）。お昼は確実に混みますので余裕を持って行ってみてね！

This is another popular restaurant you should never miss on your way back from the snow resort. Both the soup curry and the roux curry are delicious, so I can never make up my mind easily. It will definitely be crowded at lunchtime, so please go with plenty of time!

● トマム Tomamu

フルマークス トマム
FULLMARKS TOMAMU

NORRONA,HESTRA,houdiniを中心としたアウトドア系のセレクトショップ。店長はスノーボーダーで、シーズン中は毎日滑っているのでリアルなゲレンデコンディションを聞ける。ホタルストリート内にあるのでスキーインしてお食事、そしてフルマークスでギアチェック！

An outdoor select shop concentrated on NORRONA, HESTRA, and Houdini. The store manager is a snowboarder, and he snowboards every day during the season, so you can listen to realistic slope conditions. It's located on Hotaru Street, so you can ski, enjoy a nice meal, and check your gear at FULLMARKS!

● 上富良野 Kamifurano

第一食堂
Dai ichi shokudo

この街でおもいっきり親しまれている定食屋さん。おじいちゃんおばあちゃん、自衛隊、会社帰りの人でいつも大賑わい。決まって頼むのは「おかず5品定食」は、明らかに5品どころじゃなくてお腹いっぱい。

A set meal restaurant that is very popular in this town. It is always crowded with grandpas, grandmas, the Self-Defense Forces, and people returning from work. I always ask for the "five side dishes set meal," which is obviously not five dishes but more and full of satisfaction.

カネココーヒー
Kaneko Coffee Beans

上富良野で一番の人気店。コーヒーはもちろん、ボリュームのあるメニューは一度行ったら病みつきに。パティシエが作ったスウィーツも絶品です。お腹をすかして行きましょう。

The most popular restaurant in Kami-Furano. No need to mention the coffee, but you will be addicted to their hearty dishes. The sweets made by the pastry chef are also excellent. Please make sure you are hungry when you visit.

とある焼肉屋さん
A certain BBQ restaurant

「ウチはあんまりそういうのはね」やんわりと掲載を断られた焼肉屋さん。僕もあまり教えたくないから結果オーライなんですが、お肉の写真だけでも。上富良野は「豚サガリ」が有名な町。美味しい焼肉屋さんがいっぱいあるので、お気に入りのお店を見つけてみてはいかが？

"Sorry, we are not interested," he said. A Yakiniku restaurant that gently refused to be exposed in this book. I will just put a picture of the meat. Since I am also not so ready to disclose this nice restaurant, for me it is OK. Kami-Furano is a town famous for pork sagari (belly meat).

● 中富良野 Nakafamifurano

ネパールダイニング
Nepal Dining

ポカラダイニングにいたクリシュナさんが独立してオープンしたカレー屋さん。まず、間違いないです。暖かい接客でいつもまったりさせてもらってます。本場のカレーは美味いですよー。

A curry shop owned by Krishna-san, who was working at POKHARA Dining, and now went out on his own. You'll never be disappointed. I am always relaxed and stay for a while with his warm customer service. The authentic curry is delicious.

旭川
Asahikawa

東川
Higashikawa

旭川空港
Asahikawa Airport

上富良野
Kamifurano

大雪山国立公園
Daisetsuzan National Park

中富良野
Nakafurano

富良野
Furano

トマム
Tomamu

10km

関わった人物をピックアップ（フォトグラファー佐藤圭目線）　Potted Biography by Key Sato, Photographer

山木匡浩（ヤマキックス）
Tadahiro Yamaki
(yamaki-X)

プロスキーヤー。彼のマニアックな動き、大好きです。もちろんスキーはかっこいいし、スタイルもあり、なんとなく共感するもの多いなと、勝手に思い込んでいます。もっともっと山でも街でも見ていたいと思うライダー。in the PHOTO GALLERY。

Pro skier. A rider who I want to see more and more in the mountains and the city. Of course, his skiing has a cool style, and I like his maniac movements. I am somehow convinced by myself that there are many things in common that somehow sympathize with each other. Appeared in the PHOTO GALLERY.

中川伸也
Shinya Nakagawa

東川在住、山岳ガイド、プロスノーボーダー、クラフトビール作り、アイス屋さん…。肩書きはいっぱいあるけれど、何をやらせてもこなしちゃうマルチプレーヤー。ゆっくりした性格で、いつも力の抜けたライディングがクール。けどね、滑りのスイッチが入ると止められなくなる熱いライダーなのは、ここだけの話。in the PHOTO GALLERY。

A mountain guide, professional snowboarder, craft beer maker, and ice cream shop owner… who is a Higashikawa resident. A multiplayer that can handle well whatever he does. He has a relaxed personality and always has a cool riding style. However, a super-hot passionate rider who can't be stopped once his switch is turned on. Appeared in the PHOTO GALLERY.

中川未来
Miki Nakagawa

プロスキーヤー。初めて会ったのは撮影で行った上富良野の山。どんな滑りをするのかわからないので、ちょっと心配していたら、淡々とエグい斜面を何本も決めていきました。そんなミキは、今ではビックマウンテンの大会でいつも上位、というか優勝ばかり。in the PHOTO GALLERY。

Pro skier. The first time I met her, I was shooting in the backcountry of Kami-Furano. First, I was a little worried, since I didn't know her well or the style of her skiing. But she was way better than expected and skied very difficult slopes successfully in as-usual cool way. Now, she is always ranked among the top riders in the Big Mountain competition, or most of the time is winning. Appeared in the PHOTO GALLERY.

瀧久美子 Kumiko Taki

いつも元気なプロスノーボーダーくみちゃん。明日晴れるんだけど、どーかなって急なお誘いにもすぐに飛んできてくれる。マッターホルンや百名山登頂などいろんなことにアクティブで、どこに向かっているのは謎がこれからもいろんなところに連れ回したいと思っています。あ、連れ回されてるのかもですが。in the PHOTO GALLERY。

Pro snowboarder. Always cheerful, Kumi-chan. She will make herself available for a sudden invitation to a photography session. She is very active in various things, having climbed Matterhorn and hundreds of famous mountains in Japan. Although, it is always a mystery where she is heading next. I would like to continue to take her to various places—or maybe, I'm the one being taken around. Appeared in the PHOTO GALLERY.

長谷川明生 Akio Hasegawa

スキーヤーで農家。僕が出会った人の中でもかなり上位にいるスキーバカ（もちろん良い意味で）。カムイのスノードルフィン所属で、昼間はレッスン（ない時は滑りまくっている）、終わってからはサンタプレゼントパークのナイターを営業終了まで滑っている。その動きをシーズン中ずっと続けているにも関わらず、会うと疲れた顔を一切見せない、満面の笑顔が本当に気持ち良い。in the PHOTO GALLERY。

Skier and farmer. The top-ranked ski freak in my life. During the day, he will be occupied by lessons; if not, he will be enjoying his time skiing. After the school's operating hours, he will be enjoying night skiing until the end. He will be doing the same (always skiing) for the entire season, but I never see him exhausted, and his big smile is always refreshing to see. Appeared in the PHOTO GALLERY.

浅川誠
Makoto Asakawa

プロスキーヤー。僕がこの世界に入るきっかけとなった最重要人物の一人。地元旭川とスキーをこよなく愛し、我が道を貫くスタイル。生き方がカッコいい男。ずっと撮らせてもらっていますが、いつになっても目が離せないんです。

Pro skier. One of the most important people who inspired me to enter this world as photographer. A man with the best way of life and a love of his local Asahikawa and skiing. And he has his style and just goes through his way. I've been shooting for a long time, but I can't take my eyes off him.

山内一志
Kazushi Yamauchi
(Yama-chan)

プロスノーボーダー。浅川とともに僕の中での最重要人物、人呼んでオレンジマン。一目見たら忘れられない風貌と、一緒にいるだけで幸せな気分にさせてくれる平和なキャラクター。今日もどこかで、海や山で気持ちいいターンをしていることでしょう。

Pro Snowboarder. The "Orange Man," the most important person to me along with Asakawa. A peaceful character that makes you feel happy just by being with him, with an unforgettable appearance at first glance. Today, somewhere, he will be making a pleasant turn in the sea or mountains.

森島和宏
Kazuhiro Morishima

ビデオグラファー。彼がテレビ番組「ノーマター ボード」のディレクターだった時からの付き合いで、現在は「LOVE SKI HOKKAIDO」のディレクターであり、マルチなクリエーター。独特の空気感を持っていてみんなを和ませてくれています。いつも長い移動をさせちゃっているけど、これからもまだまだ動いてもらうので、よろしく！今回は黒岳撮影に参加。

Videographer. A multi-creator I have known since he was director of "NO MATTER BOARD," and now he is director of "LOVE SKI HOKKAIDO." His atmosphere compared to no others makes everyone feel at ease. he participated in Kurodake movie shooting.

野村竜　Ryu Nomura

新得のガイドカンパニーTAC代表。夏はラフティング、冬は山のガイドで年中自然の中にいる3児のスーパーパパ。甘～い笑顔と気配り満点のガイディングは、一度経験すると病みつきに！は言い過ぎかな（笑）。ガイド中いつも思うのは、「ん？一番楽しんでいるんじゃない？（笑）」本編「旅はスキーを彩る」に登場。

President of TAC. A super dad with three children, who is in nature all year round, in summer as a rafting guide and in winter as a mountain guide. His sweet smile and attentive guidance make many guests become addicted once they experience it! To exaggerate a bit, when I see him skiing after the guests, I always think "Oh, he might be the one having the most fun!". Appeared in "Travel colors skiing" section.

加藤雅明
Masaaki Kato

中富良野・ノーザン スターロッジ、オーナー。今は無きスキージャーナル誌の編集長だった頃からのお付き合いで、今では良いコンディションの山でよく会う人の1人。セルフビルドで作り上げたノーザンスターロッジは素敵すぎて大人気。

Owner of Northern star lodge. I met him as editor-in-chief of the ski magazine Ski Journal, which has been discontinued now, and now he is one of the people I often meet in the mountains in good condition. The Northern Star Lodge, which he built by himself, is so nice and very popular.

佐藤浩章
Hiroaki Sato

占冠中央スキー場勤務。パリスタート富良野・石黒さんの古くからの友人で、占冠中央スキー場を案内してくれた。今は、バックカントリースキーにハマってガイドの勉強をしている傍、ローカルゲレンデを手伝ったり、キッズの育成などにも力を入れている。

Staff of Shimukappu Chuou ski resort. A skier living in Furano, Mr. Sato is addicted to backcountry skiing and is studying as a guide while helping at the local snow resort. He is also focusing on training kids.

高山健吾
Kengo Takayama

旭岳ロープウェイに勤務し、旭岳愛がひしひしと伝わってくる古くからの友人。毎日のインスタフォトは（職権濫用で）スタッフしか絶対に撮れない写真をアップして話題に。僕が「いいね」をしないのは、見てないわけじゃなくて、ただ悔しいだけです（笑）。

An old friend of mine who works at Asahidake, and who always has a big love for Asahidake. In the daily Instagram photo that he uploads, which can only be taken by the staff, he is making some noise. The reason that I do not "like" it is just my small envy—not that I haven't seen it.

地球を滑る旅　過去の旅を一挙紹介！ Introducing Past "Ride the Earth"!

NO.1 "LEBANON"

記念すべき最初の目的地は、紛争と砂漠のイメージが先行するレバノン共和国。「そもそも雪なんてあるの？」と不安を抱いていた我々が出会ったのは、豪雪に包まれたスキー場から地中海に飛び込むような夢のロケーションだった。ハプニングとラッキーの綱渡りの連続で、奇跡とも言える滑走と旅を収めた「地球を滑る旅シリーズ」第一弾！

The first destination of the trip was the Lebanese Republic, about which you may have strong images of conflict and desert. We were worried: "Is there snow in the first place?" We met dream locations like jumping into the Mediterranean Sea from a heavy snow-surrounded ski resort. Full of happenings and lucky things, which you may find as miracles. The first in the series of "Ride the Earth."

NO.2 "MOROCCO"

大きな反響を呼んだレバノンの旅から2年。二人が向かった先は、活気と熱気に満ち溢れた大地だった。北アフリカのモロッコ共和国。海、牧草地、砂漠、煌びやかなマーケットなど、様々な色彩を見せるこの国の中央には、まるで天空をかすめるかのような巨大な山脈が横たわっている。遥か昔から交易路の難所と言われてきたアトラス山脈。そこには、世界のどことも異なる奇妙な雪が…。

In the center of the Kingdom of Morocco in North Africa, there are various landscapes such as seas, meadows, deserts, flashy markets, and a huge mountain range that looks like it is touching the sky. The Atlas Mountains, which have been long said to be a difficult trade route. There is a snow which is unique, not found anywhere else in the world…

NO.3 "ICELAND"

イギリスから大西洋を隔てた北西の果てに、躍動的な大自然に囲まれ、国民の60％以上が妖精の存在を信じている不思議な国があるという。アイスランド共和国。無数の火山、広大な氷河、無数の滝、入り組んだフィヨルド、荒れ狂うブリザード、激しくうねる海…。厳しい自然の隙間に見え隠れする妖精に導かれるように、夢に見たような斜面に遭遇するのだった。

At the northwestern end of the Atlantic Ocean, beyond England, there is a mysterious country surrounded by dynamic nature, where more than 60 percent of the population believes in the existence of fairies: the Republic of Iceland. Countless volcanoes, vast glaciers, many waterfalls, intricate fjords, raging blizzards, stormy seas… We encountered a dreamy snow mountain, guided by a fairy who appeared and disappeared in the harsh nature.

NO.4 "KASHMIR"

人間の森とも言われるインドの喧騒を抜け北へ。インド北部からパキスタン北東部にかけて広がるカシミール地方。そこは、政治と宗教間で揺れ動き、今もなお停戦状態という極めて不安定な政情にある一方で、「地上の楽園」とも称される豊かな自然が広がる地域でもある。一生で一度は絶対に滑りに行かなければならない。何かに突き動かされる自分がいた。

Go north through the hustle and bustle of India, the human forest, to the Kashmir region that spreads over from northern India to northeastern Pakistan.
Though in a truce, the political situation is still extremely unstable, swaying between politics and religion, but this area is also well known for its abundant nature, also known as "paradise on earth." I was driven by something—I must definitely go skiing there once in my lifetime.

NO.5 "RUSSIA"

世界一広く、世界一の多民族国家であるロシアは、今もなお多くの謎に包まれた国だ。そんなロシアで我々が選んだ目的地は、地理的にも文化的にも両極にある地域だった。日本から最も近い外国であり、野生の宝庫とも言われるロシア南東端のサハリン。そして、多くのミステリアスな都市伝説が伝わるロシア北西端のコラ半島。果たしてどのような出会いがあるだろうか…。

The Russian Federation, the world's largest and most multi-ethnic nation, is still a mysterious country. The destination we chose in Russia was a region that was both geographically and culturally polar. Sakhalin, the treasure trove of wildlife at the southeastern tip of Russia, is the closest foreign country to Japan. And the Kola Peninsula at the northwestern tip of Russia, where many mysterious urban legends exist. What may we encounter there??

NO.6 "GREECE"

息をのむほど青いエーゲ海の沿岸に白い家が立ち並び、道路脇にはオリーブやレモンがたわわに実っている。どんな街に出かけても古代の面影に遭遇し、ギリシャ神話に登場する神々が、今にも目の前に現れそうな神秘の国。世界中から観光客が訪れるこの国には、実はあまり知られていない、もう一つの顔がある。鮮やかな色彩に満ちた自然の中にひときわ輝く、スキーヤー・スノーボーダーを魅了する雪の楽園が存在するというのだ…。

White houses line up on the coast of the breathtaking blue Aegean Sea, and olives and lemons grow on the side of the road. A mysterious country where the gods from Greek mythology are about to appear in front of you. This country, which is visited by tourists from all over the world, has hidden charm not revealed and exposed. There is a snow paradise that fascinates skiers and snowboarders, which shines in the vibrant nature…

NO.7 "CHINA"

2022年の冬季五輪に向け、国策としてスノースポーツ人口3億人を目指し、加速する中国。資金力とエネルギーを投じて膨大な人工雪を生み出し、スキー場の規模に似合わない巨大なホテルが乱立している。このように、もっとも若いスキー大国を目指す中国だが、カザフスタンとの国境近くの山奥に、約8千年前に描かれたスキーの壁画が残されているとは…。最も若いスキーと最も古いスキーを訪ね、広大な中国を駆け回る。

The People's Republic of China is accelerating the growth of its winter sports population, aiming for 300 million as a national policy for the 2002 Winter Olympics. As it invests money and energy, a huge amount of artificial snow is produced, along with huge hotels that do not fit the scale of the snow slopes. China aims to become the youngest skiing power country, but in the mountains near the border with Kazakhstan, there are murals of skiing painted approximately twenty thousand years ago…

パウダースノー研究　星野佳路

そろそろパウダースノーの定義を世界で統一すべき時だ。近年、海外から多くのパウダーラバーが日本の雪山にいらっしゃるが、様子が変な時がある。圧雪したゲレンデに3センチの新雪が乗った斜面を滑り「ナイスパウダー」と叫んでいるかと思えば、ゲレンデの横に積み上がった雪に登り「グレートパウダー」と言っていたりする。ロサンジェルスの寿司屋で、鰻とイチゴのカリフォルニアロールに出会った時に「これを寿司と呼んで良いのか」と思う感覚に似ているのである。

そこで本日、パウダースノーを少々滑ってきた経験、そして観光のプロという視点からその定義作成を試みたい。パウダースノーとは、粉雪であるが、粉と言ってもいろいろな状態の粉があり、その要素を分解すると第1に気温、第2に積雪量、これら2つでかなり説明できるように思う。つまり気温と積雪量に基準を設定すれば、パウダースノーの質感を定義できると思うがいかがであろうか。

くだらない試みと思う諸君も多いかもしれないが、これは意外に重要なのである。例えば、ワインも味の要素を分解して言葉にし、それらを数値化している。ドライの度合いを表現して星の数を付けたりすることで消費者にとって解りやすい状態をつくり、それは市場を広げ、造り手にとっても重要な指標となった。私たちはワインを飲む時に「どの程度ドライか」と考えながら飲むようになったので「ドライで美味しい」と感じたりするのであり、そういう言葉が存在しないと、何をもって美味しいとすべきかがわからない。同じことが、多くの商品やサービスで存在している。

パウダースノーでも同じことが言えるのである。縦軸に気温、横軸に積雪量のグラフをつくるとパウダースノーの質感を5段階ぐらいで表現できるだろう。例えば、「明日朝のトマムのパウダースノーは5つ星だ」というような具合である。

こうなると、パウダースノー予報なるアプリが誕生するだろう。1つ星から5つ星までが色別になっていて、日毎そして時間ごとに各地のパウダースノー状態が刻々と変化していくのである。レストランではミシュラン3つ星レストランが最高峰であるが、日本の雪山では5つ星マウンテンが名実ともに最高峰として表示されるかもしれない。

こうすると日本の雪山のスゴさが改めて世界中に伝播されていくだろう。なぜならば、日本ほど標高が低く、駅や高速道路から近い場所で、5つ星パウダーが豊富にある場所は他にはないからだ。私は世界中で滑ることを人生のポリシーにしているのでチリやアルゼンチンでも滑ってきたが、アンデス山脈のパウダースノーの上に立った時には酸素が足りずに目眩いがしていた。コロラドのキーストーンではホテルが富士山よりも高いところにあり、一晩寝たらグループの半数が頭痛になっていた。ヨーロッパでは、標高が高い場所へのアクセスを長い年月をかけて整備し、今ではハイテクな交通手段で格好よく行くことができる。だがしかし、そういう環境に滞在するにはそれなりのコスト負担をしなければならない。

その点、日本列島は凄いのである。冬型の気圧配置が北西からの冷たい風を運び、それが海を渡る時に湿気を吸い込み、日本列島の山に当たり大量の雪を降らせる。まさに天然降雪マシーンアイランドなのである。酸素いっぱいの標高600メートル程度からパウダースノーが現れ、その周辺には街があり、文化があり、食があり、そして温泉がある。

さて、前述のパウダースノー予報アプリが完成したとしよう。その時に5つ星パウダーが最も頻繁に出現する場所が北海道の内陸（内陸はドライな雪で質が高くなる傾向にある）に位置する大雪山〜富良野〜トマムのエリアだ。この地域は頻繁に5つ星色が帯（ベルト）となって表現されるであろう。これが日本が誇るパウダーベルトだ。

世界は大観光時代に突入しようとしている。コロナ禍で一時休止したが、本格的な成長はこれからだ。パウダーベルトの凄さを表現すると人が押し寄せてしまうのではないかという懸念を持ち、嫌悪感を感じる諸君の気持ちも痛いほど解る。だがしかし、それはいずれにしても起こるのである。そうなのであれば正しく表現し、正しい評価に基づく単価を設定し、そしてオーバーツーリズムが起こらない世界最先端の施策をいち早く導入する観光先進地域になるべきだ。新しい観光の技術を活用すれば、今現在この地域の素晴らしさを静かに堪能している諸君にもプラスになる持続可能な状態を達成できるはずだ。それがこの地域の豊かな自然と誇りある地域文化を守りながら、質の高い経済を維持していく唯一の方法だと私は思う。日本には石油は出ないが雪は降るのであり、カーボンニュートラルの時代にどちらが有益かと言えばパウダースノーなのである。

Research on Powder Snow　Yoshiharu Hoshino

It is time to unify the definition of powder snow around the world. In recent years, many powder snow lovers from overseas have come to the snowy mountains of Japan. Some will scream, "Nice powder!" with three centimeters of fresh snow on a compressed slope, and some will climb to the piled snow next to the slope and say, "Great powder." The reaction to snow differs based on what they are expecting. It is like when you are faced with a California roll of eel and strawberries at a sushi restaurant in Los Angeles. You may wonder, "Can I call this sushi?"

So today, I would like to try to create a definition of powder snow from the viewpoint of a fairly experienced powder snow skier and a tourism professional. Powder snow is powdery snow. There are, however, various states of powders, which I can explain for the most part by analyzing two variables: the temperature and the amount of snow cover. In other words, if we set standards for temperature and snowfall, we can define the texture of powder snow. Many of you may think it's a silly attempt, but I believe it is surprisingly important. For example, the elements of wine's flavor can also be analyzed into words and quantified. Visualizing the degree of dryness as a number of stars made it easy for consumers to understand, which expanded the market, so it became an important index for winemakers. When we drink wine, we start to think about how dry it is, and we sometimes feel that it is dry and delicious. Without such words, we would not know what should be delicious. We can find many other products and services with similar characteristics.

The same is true for powder snow. If you make a graph with the temperature on the vertical axis and the amount of snow on the horizontal axis, you can express the texture of powder snow in about five levels. Then, you could say, "Tomorrow

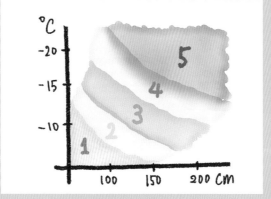

morning, Tomamu's powder snow will be five stars." When this happens, an app called "Powder Snow Forecast" will be born. The first to fifth stars will be color-coded, and the powder snow conditions in each area will change from day to day and from hour to hour. The Michelin three-star restaurant is the highest peak among restaurants, but in the snowy mountains of Japan, the five-star mountain may be displayed as the highest peak in both popularity and reality.

In this way, the greatness of Japan's snowy mountains will be spread all over the world. This is because there is no other place where the altitude is as low and the accessibility is as good, close to train stations and highways, and rich in five-star powder. My life's policy is to ski all over the world. When I have skied in Chile and Argentina and I stood on the powder snow in the Andes, I was dizzy due to the lack of oxygen. In Keystone, Colorado, the hotel was higher than Mt. Fuji, and half of the group had a headache after sleeping overnight. In Europe, access to high-altitude areas has been maintained over the years and is now well suited for high-tech transportation. However, to stay in such an environment, you have to bear a certain cost.

In that respect, the Japanese archipelago is amazing. The winter pressure distribution carries cold winds from the northwest, which inhales moisture as it crosses the sea, hitting the mountains of the Japanese archipelago and causing a large amount of snow. It is truly a natural snowfall machine. Powder snow appears from an altitude of about six hundred meters, so the air is full of oxygen, and there are towns, cultures, food, and hot springs around it.

Now, let's say the powder snow forecast app mentioned above is completed. At that time, the place where five-star powder appears most frequently is the area of Daisetsuzan-Furano-Tomamu, which is located in inland Hokkaido (the inland area tends to be of high quality due to dry snow). This area will often be represented by a five-star belt. This is the powder belt that Japan boasts to the world.

The world is about to enter an era of great tourism.

Although it was temporarily suspended due to the corona pandemic, full-scale growth is yet to come. I can understand the feelings of those who are worried and disgusted that if I express the awesomeness of the powder belt, people will rush in. But that will happen anyway. Therefore, we should become a tourism-advanced region that presents itself correctly, sets unit prices based on correct evaluations, and quickly introduces the world's most advanced measures that do not cause over-tourism. With new tourism technology, we should be able to achieve a sustainable state that will benefit those who are quietly enjoying the splendor of the region right now. I think that is the only way to maintain a strong economy while preserving the region's rich nature and proud local culture. Japan is not an oil-producing country, but we have snow. And powder snow is the most beneficial resource in the carbon-neutral era.

Kumiko Taki

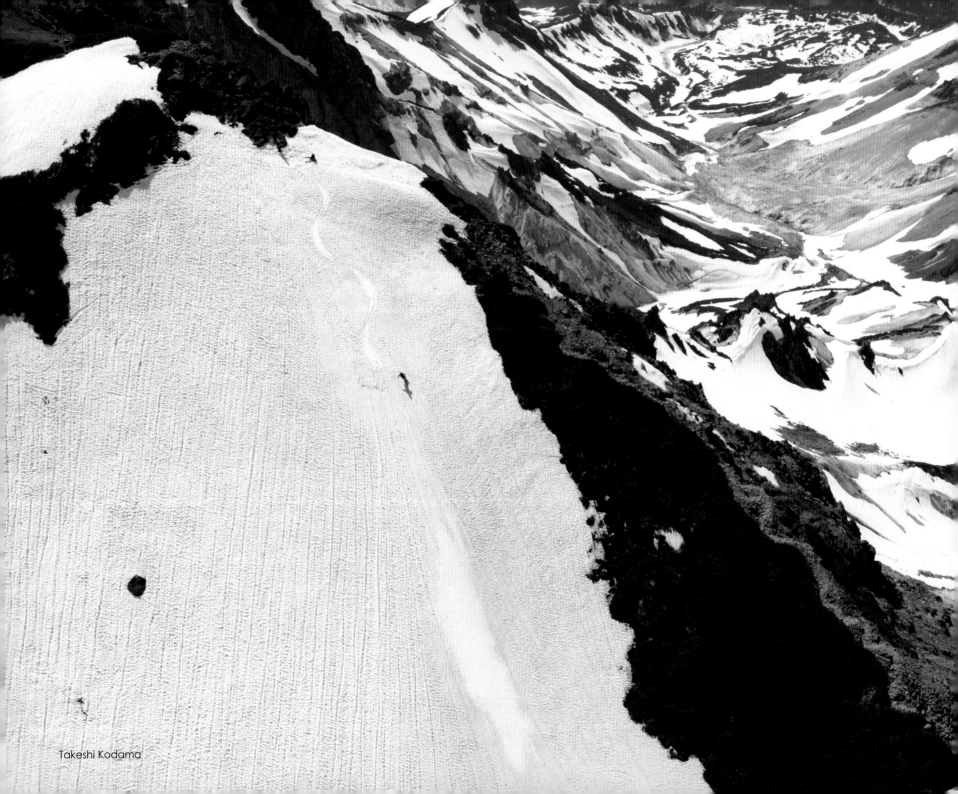

Takeshi Kodama

Akio Hasegawa

Shinya Nakagawa

Takeshi Kodama

Yuusuke Asakawa

山が開く カミホロ

早起きしてコーヒーの豆をひき、ペーパーフィルターで落とす。熱いコーヒーをすすりながら天気予報やライブカメラをチェックし、今日の行動を考える時間だ。ここ最近は、圭くんが上富良野で運営しているゲストハウス「オレンジハウス」に篭っていた。上富良野はお隣の美瑛や富良野に比べて観光のイメージが薄いので、宿と言ってもピンと来ない人が多いと思う。しかし、上富良野から十勝岳温泉まで車で20分、富良野スキー場も30分、旭岳やトマムも1時間程度という、レンタカーやマイカーさえあれば恵まれすぎた立地なのだ。オレンジハウスの隣には、道民の心の友であるセイコーマートがあり、正面にはホームセンターとドラッグストア、歩いて数分の距離にフラヌイ温泉や居酒屋、ラーメン屋、ラベンダーが綺麗な日の出公園がある。これだけ揃っていて、何で流行っていないかが不思議な宿なのだ（圭くん、失礼！）。共有スペース兼、圭くんのリビングには大きな書棚があり、スキーの古い本や旅の本が並んでいる。ここにいると不思議なくらい山の話や旅の話で盛り上がり、気づけば出発が遅れてしまうことが多々あるので要注意だ。
「この前行った三峰山下のテラスでさぁ…」早速始まった圭くん節に対し「そっか～。やっぱりいいね～」と相槌をうつ俺といういつもの構図。圭くんのカミホロ愛に耳を傾けながら、上富良野に来ている

ことを実感していた。その愛たるや、付き合い始めの高校生カップルのようなもので、時間さえ許せば山にいる。昨日良かったと思えば今日もいる。昨日悪かったけど今日もいる…という感じで、もはや病気として診断されるくらいの好きさ加減なのだ。（しかも車のナンバーが三峰山の標高だし…笑）
圭くんがまだプロカメラマンじゃなかった頃、安政火口から上富良野岳方面に登り詰めて、アルパインな雰囲気たっぷりの八ツ手岩脇の斜面を繰り返し滑っていたという。その景観と雪質に惚れ込んだ圭くんは、ある日、安政火口で幻の蝶々に出会った。それ以降、圭くんはこの場所を「ネバーランド」と呼び、永遠なる憧れの場所としてきた。世界中の未知なる雪山を旅して、即興的に写真を撮ってきた「地球を滑る旅」とは対極と言ってもいい撮影スタイルが、実は圭くんのベースにあるのだ。

1月～2月にかけて、大雪山や十勝連峰には深々と雪が降り、一度荒れ始めれば生命の存在を拒絶するような非情な山に変貌する。日照時間も短く、山での行動は様々な条件で制限される時期だ。しかし、3月に入ると山は少しずつ表情を変え、晴天率が高くなり日照時間も長くなると、雪の下地が締まってくる。マイナス20度を下回っていた

気温も緩み、長時間快適に雪山で過ごせる日が増えてくるのだ。厳冬期にたっぷりと降り積もった雪は、山全体をしっかりと包み込み、雪質も安定してくることで山での行動範囲が一気に広がってくるのもこの時期だ。このように、バックカントリースキーヤーにとって、山に入り易くなる時期になることを、俺はこう言っている。
「山が開く」と。
リフトやスノーキャットを有効活用し、時にはハイクアップして、極上のパウダースノーをとにかくたくさん滑りたい。これが一般的なスキーヤーの欲求だと思う。しかし、真の喜びはこの先なのだ。バックカントリースキーをやっていて「山が開く」ことの喜びを実感してしまうと、その人のこれからの人生が心配になるくらい、山の世界に魅了されてしまうのだ。現に、大学時代に「山が開く」つまり「山での自由」を知ってしまった俺が、その後、どのような人生を辿ったかは、冒頭に綴った自己紹介のとおりだ。まぁ、これが良いと思ったら、他のことが何もできなくなる俺を例にあげるのも極端な話だけど、スキーによって「山が開く」ことを知ることは、ある意味麻薬に手を出してしまうような危うさを内包した魅力に触れてしまうことなのだ。このようなスキーの魅力というか、魔力に取り憑かれてしまった人は、世の中にそうそういるものではないと思うのだが、俺の周りに

Mountains' acceptance Kamihoro

Wake up early in the morning, grind coffee beans, and brew coffee with a paper filter.
It's time to think about what I will do today, checking the weather forecast and live camera and enjoying hot coffee.
Recently, I was staying at the guest house "Orange House" that Key owns in Kami-Furano.
Kami-Furano has a lesser view of sightseeing spots than the neighboring Biei and Furano. Therefore, the inn at Kami-Furano may have unpopular image. However, Kami-Furano is a blessed area if you have a rental car or your own car to travel. It is a twenty-minute drive from Kami-Furano to Tokachidake Onsen and a thirty-minute drive from Furano Ski Resort. Asahidake and Tomamu are also about an hour away.
In Key's living room, which also serves as a common space and accommodation facility, there is a large bookshelf where old ski books and travel books are lined up. When I've been there, many times I have been so excited to talk about mountains and trips that I delayed my departure.
This time, as usual, Key's love of Kamihoro started to be exposed. And this usual ritual made me at home in Kami-Furano.
Key: "On the terrace at the bottom of Mt. Mitsumine, there was…"
Takeshi: "Yes, it is always a great place…"
His love of Kamihoro is like that of a high school couple who just started

dating. They will be together as much as possible if time permits. And Key will be in the mountains whenever his time allows. Like, he is there when conditions are good, but he is still there today when they're bad. Or it was bad weather yesterday, but he is still there today. His love of the mountains is sick.
Here is the story I would like to share…
Before he became a professional photographer, he often climbed from the Ansei Crater toward Mt. Kamifurano and many times enjoyed the snow of Yatsuteiwa-waki, which is full of alpine atmosphere. He fell in love with the landscape and the quality of the snow, and one day he met a rare butterfly at the Ansei Crater. Since then, Key has called this place "Neverland" and has made it his everlasting longing. The style of shooting which is Key's base is quite opposite to that of the "Ride the Earth" project. In "Ride the Earth," Key was traveling unknown snowy mountains all over the world with me and shooting extraordinary photos of what we had encountered.

From January to February, it snows deeply on Daisetsuzan and the Tokachi mountain range, and once it begins to get rough, it transforms into a ruthless mountain that refuses all life the right to exist. However, in March, the mountain gradually changes its expression, and when the proportion of sunny weather grows larger and the days become longer, the snow base

becomes tighter. The temperature, which was below -20 degrees Celsius, will become higher, and the number of days when you can spend a long time comfortably in the snowy mountains will increase.
"Mountains' acceptance" is what I call the time when it will be easier for backcountry skiers to enter the mountains.
Many skiers want to make effective use of lifts and snow cats, hike just a little, and ski as much of the finest powder snow as possible in the midwinter. But true blessed moments go beyond that. When you truly understand the joy of this "mountains' acceptance" in backcountry skiing, you will be fascinated by the mountain world, and your life will be different forever. As I mentioned in my self-introduction at the beginning, I faced this "mountains' acceptance" that is "freedom in the mountains" in my college years; since then, you know what kind of life I have followed.
Skiing is the ticket to receive this "mountains' acceptance." It is in a sense the same as if you were messing around with drugs, became strongly addicted, and could not forget and live without them.
This year, I met the person who was closest to my "mountains' acceptance" value.

I had heard about him for years from various people. A snowboarder who had been snowboarding on Asahidake for a long time, and who had

は結構いる(笑)。ヤマキックスなんかが同じ穴のムジナだと思うが、それぞれ価値観が違って面白い。そんな折、俺の価値観に最も近い人物に出会った。

彼のことは、いろいろな人から間接的に聞いていた。古くから旭岳を滑っていたスノーボーダーであり、旭川発のローカルブランド「FieldEarth」を生み出した張本人。本村勝伯さん(モトさん)。実は、ブランドとして「地球を滑る旅」をサポートしてくれているのだが、今まで一度もお会いすることがなかった。東川や富良野でイベントをやった時も来場したことがなかったので、圭くんは「モトちゃんは大勢の人が集まる場所が苦手みたいなんだよね」と言っていた。俺の中で、モトさんは「クールでちょっと哲学的な方」というイメージだった。山で初めて一緒になったモトさんは、アークテリクスのウェアをシャキッと身に纏い、エアバッグを含む完璧な装備で現れた。バラクラバで肌の隙間さえ見せない完璧な日焼け対策。濃いめのミラーレンズのゴーグルをつけているので、その表情を伺い知ることができない。やはり、モトさんと俺はタイプの違う人間なのだろう。よく晴れ渡った上ホロのD尾根をシュカブラを踏みしめながら思い思いのペースで登っていく。昨日まで爆風が吹いていたので風の影響を受けて

いない斜面を求めて歩き回ったけど、風が巻いていたせいか、この山域全体が波状にウィンドパックされた斜面になっていた。モトさんとはあまり会話するムードではなかったけど、2本滑るうちに彼の山での佇まいがとても気になるようになった。感情を表面に出さないけれど、その歩き方一つ、無線でのやりとり一つ、ライディング一つに滲み出るものがある。
「この人は、本当に山が好きで、スノーボードが好きなんだ」
何だかどんどん興味が湧いてきて、俺はいつの間にかモトさんにあれこれ質問を投げかけていた。最初に描いていたクールな哲学者タイプというイメージが、どうだろうか。スノーボードにハマったのも、スノーボードブランドを始めたのも思いつきだったらしく、「ただ、自分がやりたいことをやってきただけ」という無計画タイプだったのだ。最近始めたという趣味のトライアスロンも、笑っちゃうくらい思いつきだし、スノーボードを作るストーリーにしても「ただ乗ってみたいものを作ってみた」という超シンプルなものだった。「ただやりたいことをやっていたら、あとで周りがついてきた」という話はたまに聞くけれど、掘り下げてみると細かな苦労話がザクザクと出てくるものだ。しかし、モトさんの場合はそれが全くなく、屈託ない精神で山やスノーボードに向かっているだけだった。いろいろ話している

うちに、モトさんも俺が同類なタイプだと気づいたらしく、会話は限度なく盛り上がっていった。しまいにはモトさんが一言、「タケちゃんも、夢の叶え方知っている人でしょ?」と言った。俺の脳味噌に電流が走った。「タケちゃんも宇宙人なんでしょ?」と言われたような衝撃だったのだ。
──ヤバい! この人も、相当イッちゃってる(笑)!
人は外観や物腰だけでは判断できない。何とも、クールと思っていたモトさんの内面は、超絶アツい情熱家だったのだ。
「タケちゃんとモトちゃんを合わせたいって、ずっと思っていたんだよね」と圭くんが満足そうな表情で言った。圭くんが接着剤になってくれることで、ジャンルを超えて様々なセッションを経験してきた。いつも一緒に活動する身近な人だから見落としがちだけど、圭くんがスノー業界に与えた影響は、実は物凄く大きいと思うのだ。

established a local brand, "Field Earth," from Asahikawa. Actually, as a brand, they supported "Ride the Earth," but I had never met him before. Even at the event we had at Higashikawa and Furano, I hadn't had the privilege of meeting him. When Key informed me that he would not show up, he was explaining to me that "Moto-chan doesn't like the place where a lot of people gather." For me, Moto-san had the image of being "cool and a little philosophical."
It was finally time to meet, and Moto-san, who was with us for the first time in the mountains, wore Arc'teryx clothing crisply and appeared with perfect equipment, including an airbag. Perfect sun protection that didn't even show gaps of his skin like with a balaclava. He was wearing dark mirror-lens goggles, so I couldn't tell what he looked like. At that time, I was thinking Moto-san and I were probably different types of people, since he was so perfect.
We climbed the well-cleared Sunny D ridge of Kami-Horo, stepping on wind ripples each at his own pace. Since the blast had been blowing until yesterday, we walked around in search of a slope that had not been affected, but the entire mountain area was a wavy wind-packed slope because of the circulated wind.
I wasn't in the mood to talk to Moto-san, but as we shared slopes twice, I started to be attracted by his appearance on the mountain.

Although he didn't reveal his emotions, there was something that oozed out in his way of walking, in his radio communication, and the way he rode.
"This person really loves mountains, and he loves snowboarding."
I could not hold in my interest and started to ask Moto-san questions, to learn whether my first impression of him as a cool philosopher type was right or wrong.
As my questions went by, I understood that he had started snowboarding without thinking deeply, then got addicted and started a snowboard brand. He was an unplanned type who said, "I just did what I wanted to do." While we were taking about his story, the recent hobby, triathlon, which he had also started without thinking deeply, came up with a laugh. Even the story of making a snowboard was super simple: "I just made something I wanted to ride." I sometimes hear the story that "if I was just doing what I wanted to do, the people around me would follow me later," but most of the time when I delve into it, the details of the hardships come out a lot. However, in the case of Moto-san, there was no such thing, just finding out his pure love of the mountains and snowboarding. While talking about various things, Moto-san seemed to notice that I was the same type, and the conversation was lively, going on and on.
In the end, Moto-san said this:
"Take-chan is also a person who knows how to make his dreams come true,

right?"
An electric current ran through my brain. It was a shock, as if I had been told, "Take-chan is also an alien like me, right?"
A person cannot judge only by appearance and demeanor. The inside of Moto-san, who I thought was cool, turned out to be as super-passionate hot-blooded person.
"I've always wanted to combine Take-chan and Moto-chan," Key said with a satisfied expression.
Key has been connecting me with various people, and I have experienced diverse shooting sessions across categories. It's easy to overlook this because he's a familiar person who always works with me. I think Key's influence on the snow industry is actually enormous.

旅はスキーを彩る 屈足湖、吹上温泉、旭川

かれこれ40年以上スキーを続けているけれど、何でこんなにも楽しくて、全く飽きる気配がないのだろうか？ 冷静になって考えてみた。まず、スキー自体の魅力や奥の深さは言うまでもないけど、一番の理由は、スキーという遊びは滑ることだけではなく、旅行とセットになるからだと思うのだ。スキーをする時、大抵はマイカーや電車、飛行機、船、あるいは自転車や徒歩といった移動、つまり旅を伴う。同時に道中や滞在中に出会う人々や、景色、文化、食事…など、ありとあらゆるものが付いてくる。旅とスキーが区切られることはなく、スキートリップとして楽しまれる。「地球を滑る旅」を始めたのは、まさに、スキーが旅を面白くし、旅がスキーを面白くするからだ。俺にとって、スキートリップはどんな旅行よりもクリエイティブでエキサイティングなのだ。

厳冬期のある日、「スキーで温泉まで滑り込むストーリーで遊んでみよう」と圭くんに提案した。こんな何でもない遊びが、温泉を彩り、スキーを彩り、印象深いものになる。またある時は、「真冬の寒さを思いっきり体感しようよ」と、友人が運営するサウナ＆アヴァント（フィンランドサウナ）を体験しにいった。
「お〜う、たけちゃん。もうサウナ、バッチリ仕上がっているよ」

サウナ小屋から出てきた竜ちゃん（野村竜介）が、全身から湯気を立ち上らせて言った。大雪山系から注ぐ清流が集まって十勝平野に流れ込む場所に、屈足湖という人造湖がある。竜ちゃんは、この湖と十勝川上流を使ったラフティングなどのアクティビティを運営する十勝アドベンチャークラブ（TAC）の代表だ。割と近くにサホロやトマムというリゾートがあり、道東で2番目に人口が多い帯広市から近いこともあり、たくさんの利用者で賑わっている。しかし、コロナ禍によって状況は一転。夏も冬も閑古鳥が鳴く我慢の1年を強いられてきたのだった。だが、そんな状況に指を咥えている竜ちゃんではない。地元の魅力発見！ というばかりに地域の仲間と協力し、この土地の恵みである「寒さ」を利用した新たなアクティビティを準備していた。それが、氷結した屈足湖と、隣接する温泉施設をうまく利用した、サウナ＆アヴァントのサービスだった。屋外に設置されたサウナ小屋は約70度でいい感じに仕上がっていた。檜の香りが漂う心地よいサウナで、じっくり時間をかけて汗をかいていく。時折、TACのスタッフが頃合いを見計らってロウリュをしてくれた。「いち、に〜、サウナ〜！」と口にするのは照れくさいけれど、なんか妙な一体感があって悪くない気がしてきた。

「よし！」意を決して外に出たが、温まり方が甘かったのか、湖までの坂道を歩く間にちょっと肌寒いくらいになってしまった。俺は踵を返して再びサウナへ。2回目もやはり移動しているうちに冷めてしまったが、もう決心はついていた。真っ白く氷結した湖面に1m四方で切り取られたプール。その中に飛び込み、ワカサギとお友達になろうとしている。ワカサギの場合は釣り上げられた後に凍り付いてしまうけれど、俺は大丈夫だろうか？ どんなに燃え上がるほど熱しても一瞬にして凍えるのは、27年前に行ったシベリアのサウナで痛いほど経験していた。いかに何も考えずに飛び込むかがポイントだ。その心構えは、クリフジャンプの恐怖を克服したときに良く似ていた。具体的に言うと、「いっせーのーで」で飛び込むとしたら、普通は「で」で飛び込むけれど、「せ」で飛び込むイメージだ。後先考えずに行動なのだ！
「いっせ！」
ドボン！ という音と共に、一瞬にしてサウナでの熱帯の記憶はかき消された。心臓が困惑してパフパフと鼓動している。感じるのは寒さとか冷たさではなく、痛さと痺れだ。「コノママデハシンデシマウ」と危険信号を感知し、脳味噌でサイレンが響いている。呼吸が早くなっているのに呼吸困難。そして瞳孔が開いているのがわかる。カッコつけて温泉でも浸かっているような心地良い笑顔でもしようと思って

Travel colors skiing Kuttari Lake, Fukigami hot spring, Asahikawa

I've been skiing for over 40 years now, but why is it so much fun and never get bored?
First of all, there are no question about the ultimate charm and depth of skiing itself, I think the main reason is that skiing is not just about skiing, but also about traveling.
Skiing usually involves traveling by car, train, plane, boat, and some time biking and walking. Also the people you meet along the way and during your stay, the scenery, the culture, the food, and so on, all come together. Travel and skiing are not separated and are enjoyed as ski trips.

We started "Ride the Earth" because skiing makes traveling interesting, and traveling makes skiing interesting. Ski trips are more creative and exciting to me than any trip.

One day in the midwinter, I suggested to Key, "Why don't we do the story of skiing to the hot springs." This kind of nonsense play colors the hot springs, skis, and makes strong impression.
On another occasion, I said, "Let's experience the cold of midwinter to the fullest" and went to experience the Sauna and Avant (Finnish sauna) run by a friend while skiing.
"Hi Take-chan, the sauna is ready completely."

Ryu-chan, who came out of the sauna hut, said and the steam was rising from the whole body.
There is an artificial lake called Kuttari Lake in the place where the clear streams pouring from the Daisetsu Mountains gather and flow into the Tokachi Plain. Ryu-chan is the representative of the Tokachi Adventure Club (TAC), which manages activities such as rafting using this lake and the upper reaches of the Tokachi River. There are resorts such as Sahoro and Tomamu relatively close to it, and it is close to Obihiro City, which is the second most populous city in Eastern Hokkaido, so it is crowded with many users. However, the situation changed due to the corona pandemic. In both summer and winter, he was forced to endure a year of quiet and slow in business.

However, Ryu-chan is not a person who look enviously in such a situation. 'Discover the charm of the local area!' slogan, he was preparing a new activity using the 'cold' that is the blessing of this land in cooperation with local colleagues. That was the service of Sauna & Avant, which made good use of the frozen Kuttari Lake and the adjacent hot spring facility. The outdoor sauna hut was prepared nicely at about 70 degrees (Celsius) .
I slowly sweat in a comfortable sauna with the scent of cypress.
Occasionally, the TAC staff did the löyly (throwing water on hot stones in sauna) at the right time. It's embarrassing to say "Ichi , ni ~, sauna ~!" (this was the call we were asked from staffs), but I feel that it's not bad because there is a strange sense of unity.
I made up my mind to go outside saying "OK!", but maybe I was not warm enough, it became a little chilly while walking down the path to the lake. I turned my heels back and went to the sauna again. The second time, after all, it got cold while I was moving, but I was already determined. I was jumping into a pool cut out in 1m square on the surface of the frozen lake and trying to become friends with Wakasagi (smelt).
In smelt fishing, in case of smelt, it freezes after being caught, but am I OK??
I've already have experienced in Siberian sauna, no matter how hot you burns in the sauna, you will freeze instantly when you go outside.
In this kind of occasion, the point is how to jump in without thinking. The attitude was very similar when I overcame the fear of cliff jumping.
"Yes!"
With the noise of my splash, the memory of the hot sauna was drowned out in an instant. My heart is confused and beating. I don't feel cold or chill, but pain and numbness. Detecting a danger signal, a siren is echoing in my brain. Even though I am breathing faster, I have difficulty breathing. And I feel my pupil open. I was thinking of pretend pleasantly and smile as if I

いたけれど、溺れているような必死の顔しかできず、生命を維持するための本能だけで動いていた。
「だあああ！！」
水から上がると、さらに強烈な寒さが襲ってきた。体の表面が凍ってくるのがわかるのだ。
「ひいいいぃ！！」
27年前から何にも成長してないじゃねーか！（笑）しかし、体をタオルでしっかり拭いてみると、あら不思議。地獄のような寒さから解放されて感覚が麻痺したのか？ 何となく身体がポカポカして、頭はスッキリしている。そして、変なアドレナリンが出てコーフンしていた。ちょっと違う気もするけれど、これが「整った」と言うことなのだろうか？ もしかして、結構、癖になるかも！！

was soaking in a hot spring, in reality I could only make a desperate face like I am drowning. I was moving with my instinct to maintain my life.
"Nooo!!"
When I got out of the water, an even more intense cold struck me. I can feel that the surface of my body freezes.
"Oh my God!"
However, when I wiped my body with dry towel, 'hey presto'. May be sense was paralyzed by the hellish coldness. Somehow my body is warm and my head is clear.   And I was excited and feeling adrenaline flow in my blood stream.
I think it's a little different, but is this what it means to be "ready"?
I am starting to love sauna.

新しい体験に気をよくした俺たちは、旭川の街に繰り出した。旭川の中心部は高いビルが少なく、どこからでも大雪山系を望むことができる。駅前にステイしていても、車を発進すればすぐに郊外に出ることができるし、空港やスキー場も近く、バスで行き来することもできる。そして、ホテルから徒歩圏内に美味しい飲食店が無数にあるのだ。旭川自体には大きなスキー場がないので、スキーのイメージがない人が多いと思うけど、アプレスキーも含めてトータルでバランスが良く、ステイするには便利な場所だ。なるほど、世界で一番滑る社長を目指しているという某フルマークスの社長が通いつめる(入り浸る?)のも納得と言う感じなのだ。雪が積もった小路には、提灯がともった場末感漂う小さな店が軒を連ねており、演歌が似合いそうな老舗もあれば、若者が集う小洒落たカフェバーもある。極寒の地の酒場というのは、妙にホッとさせてくれる場所だ。

俺には「スキーに良い場所には決まって美味しい食べ物と美味しいお酒がある」という持論がある(またしても偏見だが)。多分、滑った後は食事やお酒が10割増しで美味しく感じる効果が影響しているとは思うけど、俺は改めてスキーという遊びが旅や飲食と相性が良すぎることに感動していた。地球を滑る旅の一回目で行ったレバノンの時は、圭くんと一日を乾杯で締めくくるのが恒例だった。お酒に関しては健康面とか人によって考え方は様々だけど、俺は賛成派であり推進派だ。「乾杯」は、単に飲み始めるための号令にあらず。

今日一日に感謝し、お互いの存在を祝福し合う分かりやすい行為が好きだ。当然、お酒自体が美味しいし、奥が深くて面白い。お酒によって食事が美味しくなるのも素晴らしい。最近、圭くんが「俺、別に飲まなくてもいいな」と言うので、「失礼しまーす…」と言って一人で飲むことが多くなった。圭くんが沢山飲んでいたイメージは、それこそロシア人とボーリングをしながらウォッカを一気飲みして以来ないかも？あの時、酷い二日酔いで行った撮影のトラウマが影響しているのか？とにかく俺は、圭くんがこちら側(のんべえサイド)に帰ってくることを気長に待ち続けている。

この本で、北海道の雪がいかに良いのかをウザイくらいに語ってきたけれど、アプレスキーの要素を加えると、「世界中のスキーヤーが北海道に来たがるに決まってる！」と言い切っても良いくらいだ。温泉や観光などもあるけれど、中でも大きな要素が食事ではないだろうか。美味しくてヘルシーで繊細で美しい日本料理はもちろん、日本人は世界中の料理をさらに美味しくアレンジし、最終的には家庭料理にまで取り入れてしまうという、素晴らしい才能を持っている。それに加えて、新鮮で質の高い山海の幸に恵まれ、大雪山などから渾々と湧き出る天然水に恵まれた土地なのだ。これだけ要素が揃って食事が美味しくないわけはない。これが、スキー場がある国々の基準で言えばかなり安価で食すことができるのだ。ヨーロッパのリゾートに行ったとき、安めのお店で軽食を摘んだだけで3,000円

かかったけれど、旭川の街なら3,000円あれば美味しいものを飲んで食べてお釣りが来るくらいなのだ。
自分がもしも日本人以外のスキーヤーに生まれて「地球を滑る旅」をしたいと思ったとしたら…。旅先の筆頭に「日本」が来て、その行き先に北海道を選ぶだろう。スキートリップに行く動機付けとして、全てが揃っている場所。世界の隅々からこの地に人が訪れることの意味を我々道産子は理解しているようでまだまだ足りないと思うのだ。
「まったくもう、なんて最高なんだ…」
俺は、皿に残っていたひと欠けの新子焼を口に放り込むと、よく冷えたビールをグビグビと煽った。

We were happy with the new experience and went out to the city of Asahikawa. There are few tall buildings in the center of Asahikawa, and you can see the Daisetsu Mountains from anywhere. Even if you are staying in front of the station, you can go out to the suburbs very soon if you get in your car, and the airport and ski resort are nearby, so you use the bus for transportation. And there are countless delicious restaurants within walking distance of the hotel. Asahikawa itself doesn't have a big ski resort, so I think many people don't have the image of skiing, but it's a convenient place to stay because it's well-balanced in total, including the après-ski. The snow-covered alley is lined with small shops with lanterns; some of them look good on enka (Japanese country-style songs very traditional old Japanese style), and some of them are stylish cafe bars where young people gather. A bar in a frigid place is a strangely relieving place.

Going back to après-ski, I think there are always good food and good drinks in good places for skiing. Perhaps the effect of eating and drinking after skiing is many times more delicious; I was once again impressed by the fact that skiing is very compatible with travel, eating, and drinking.

And beyond the delicious, healthy, delicate, and beautiful Japanese food we already have, the Japanese have a wonderful talent for arranging dishes from all over the world even more deliciously and eventually incorporating them into home cooking. In addition to our talent as foodies, Asahikawa is blessed with fresh and high-quality seafood and mountain-based foodstuffs, and natural water that springs up from Daisetsuzan. Food cannot be more delicious than in Asahikawa with all these elements. And you can enjoy this good food at a fairly inexpensive price compared to the standards of the countries where ski resorts are located. When I went to a resort in Europe, it cost me three thousand yen just to pick up a light meal at a non-luxurious shop, but in the city of Asahikawa, if it's three thousand yen, I can drink and eat delicious food and I may still get some change.

If I was born as a non-Japanese skier and wanted to do the same project "Ride the Earth," I would pick Japan as the first country to visit, and Hokkaido would be selected as the destination.

For me, Hokkaido is a place where everything is available to motivate me. It seems that we Dosanko (a horse native to Hokkaido, often used to refer to the people of Hokkaido) understand the meaning of people coming to Hokkaido from every corner of the world, but I think we have more to study and understand.

"What a wonderful place…"

I threw a piece of shinkoyaki (roasted chicken) left on the plate into my mouth and finished my cold beer.

残雪を追いかけて 黒岳

北海道の春は、俺に言わせると必要以上に足早に訪れる。いや、そんなに早く訪れていないのに、長い冬が終わるのを待ちわびた人々がフライングして、季節以上に春っぽさを求めるのだ。特にイラつくのは、放っておいても解ける軒先の氷を一日中割っている人だ。俺なんて、家の雪が解けるのが勿体無くて、絶対に割ったり広げたりしないのに、それでもあっけなく解けてしまうのだ。どうせ解ける氷をわざわざ割っている時間と元気があるんだったら、春山に遊びに行こうぜ〜！と言いたいところだけど、これは真冬のスキー以上に理解されない（笑）。現に、5月になっても毎日スキーウェアを着て出ていく俺を、近所の人たちが不思議そうに見ているし、息子たちだって「まだ滑れるの？」と本気で驚いている。確かに、街は新緑や花々で色づき、冬の間は出来なかったことが出来るようになる季節。入学式や入社式など、新しいスタートを切る時期とも重なり、みんな新しいことに目が移りがちだ。「まだスキーなんてしているの？」と言われることがあるけれど、俺はこれに対して全力で反論したい。残雪スキーは真冬のスキーと全く違った魅力を持った、サイコーにエキサイティングで、サイコーに快感な遊びだということ！ つまり、5月のゴールデンウィークの後のシーズンは、しぶとくスキーにしがみついているシーズンではない！ 新しい遊びがスタートするシーズンなのである！

車の中にはスキーが数本、キャンプ用具、釣竿、山菜採りのセット、自転車、トレランシューズ、SUP…。季節は夏に向かっていくけれど、スキーが終わるシーズンはもう少し先なので、遊び道具の種類が日に日に増えていって大変なことになっている。
「おお〜、すっかり景色が変わったな〜」
災害級の積雪だった（2021年）岩見沢も、雪の欠片すらなく綺麗に解けきり、新緑の時期を過ぎて濃厚な緑の時期に突入していた。鳥たちや虫の鳴き声は大きく、雪解けで増水していた川の濁流も、透き通った清流に戻りつつある。こうなると、残された雪の楽園はかなり限定されてくる。もともと、北海道には残雪スキーのメッカが存在しない。北海道民は春になるとスキーからグリーンシーズンの遊びに移行してしまうのが一番の理由だ。道外だと、立山、月山、鳥海山、乗鞍高原、千畳敷など、ロープウェイや観光道路で残雪までアプローチでき、周辺に宿泊施設があるエリアがあるけれど、北海道の場合は、この時期になるとロープウェイがメンテナンス期間に入ったり、観光道路もわざわざ除雪しない。したがって、我々は、遥かなる雪山をスキーを背負い、時には自転車で、時には登山道をよっこらよっこら歩いてアプローチしなければならない。う〜ん、やっぱり流行らないかも（笑）。

夏リフト営業初日。例年ならたくさんの春スキー愛好家で溢れる黒岳だが、コロナ禍の影響で静まり返っていた。それでも、朝6時から営業を開始してくれていることが有り難く、俺たちは、係の人たちに一礼して、ロープウェイに乗り込んだ。ロープウェイは、濃緑の山肌を這うように登っていき、次第に展望が開けてきた。そして、深い黒岳沢の向こうにたっぷりと残雪をたたえた上川岳の姿が見えてきた。今日は、天候と残雪の量さえ許せば、あの大斜面を滑りたいと思っていた。ポカポカ陽気の中、リフトに乗り継ぎ、手際良くハイクアップの準備を済ませると、雪解けが進んで毛羽立った雪面を、一歩一歩確かめるように登り始めた。黒岳山頂への急坂を登っていると、いつも思い出すことがある。あれは今から25年前、バックカントリースキーを始めたばかりの大学3年の春のことだ。

「よし！ 行こうぜ！」
昨年スキーを始めたばかりの大学の親友、イシカワ（石川大輔）と一緒に黒岳山頂を目指していた。ゴアテックスの存在すら知らなかった俺たちは、どう見ても山のドシロウトで、綿がたっぷりと入ったスキーパンツにジージャンという舐めきった出で立ち。
「この前見たモーグルのビデオに出てた人が、ジージャンで滑ってて

Chasing the remaining snow Kurodake

Spring in Hokkaido comes faster than necessary, if you ask me. Well, people who have been waiting for the end of a long winter are seeking more springiness, though spring itself has not come.
Neighbors are quizzically looking at me wearing ski suits every day even in May, and even my sons are really surprised, asking me, "Can you still ski?" Certainly, the city is colored with fresh greenery and flowers starting to bloom, and it is a season when you can do things that you could not do during the winter. In Japan, April is a startup season, with the school entrance ceremony; new graduates start working; everyone tends to shift their eyes to new things. Sometimes people ask me, "Are you still skiing?" But I want to argue against this question with all my might.
The remaining snow season has a completely different charm from midwinter skiing—it is exciting and pleasant play in the mountains. So, the season after Golden Week (a week of national holidays in beginning May) in May isn't the season to cling to skiing! It's the season when new play starts!

There were several skis in my car, fishing rods, tools for picking edible wild plants, bicycles, trail running shoes, and SUP. As the season headed towards summer, and the end of skiing season was a little ways away, the variety of my goods was increasing day by day, which was creating a big mess in my car.

"Wow, the scenery has changed completely."
In Iwamizawa, where they had had a disaster-grade snowfall this past winter, the snow had melted cleanly without a trace, and the city had entered the rich green season after the fresh green season.
Birds and insects screamed, and the muddy stream of the river, which had been bit flooded by the thaw, was returning to a clear stream. When this has happened, the remaining snow paradise is quite limited.
Originally, there was no popular place for the remaining snow skiing in Hokkaido. The main reason is that the people of Hokkaido shift from skiing to playing in the green season in the spring. Outside of Hokkaido, you can approach the remaining snow on ropeways and sightseeing roads in such places as Mt. Tateyama, Mt. Gassan, Mt. Chokai, Norikura Kogen, and Senjojiki, and there are areas with accommodation facilities in the vicinity. In the case of Hokkaido, the ropeway enters the maintenance period at this time, and the tourist road does not bother to remove snow. Therefore, we carry skis on the distant snowy mountains, sometimes by bicycle, sometimes by walking on mountain trails.
Hmmm, it may not become popular after all…

Kurodake, which would start its summer lift business from today, started business at 6 a.m. even though there were few customers due to the influence of COVID-19. As the ropeway climbed the dark green mountain surface, the view opened at once, and I could see Kamikawadake with plenty of snow behind the deep Kurodakezawa. Today, I wanted to ski on that big slope, if the weather and the amount of snow left allowed. I started to hike and let the crampons bite into the rough slopes of spring.
The duo of the metallic sound of crampons' clatter and the crisp sound of blades biting into the rough snow echoed in the windless mountains.
Looking back while enjoying the comfortable slope to immerse myself in the climb, the two photographers carrying heavy luggage had almost stopped.
Basically, I never see Key climbing comfortably. He may have a backache, a shoulder-ache, difficulty with physical fitness or heat. With all these challenges, I never see him compromise his equipment due to any of these factors.
Just as we have an overflowing desire to "ski!", Key's desire to "take a good picture!" is extraordinary.
And it's same for Morishi, a video cameraman who accompanied us today. He had driven a long distance at midnight, carried a big tripod and a huge backpack, and accompanied a skier for a shoot that may not be a job for him.
I'm really blessed—that's what I thought.

「さぁ、なまらカッコ良かったから俺も着てきちゃったぜ！」…我ながらアホである。

さらには、恐ろしく重いレーシングブーツを履き、スクールの倉庫で拾った2mの細板を背負ってのツボ足スタイルだった。今、俺がそんな人を見かけたら、「そんな格好で山に入ったら遭難するよ」と声をかけるところだ。豊富な残雪を誇る大雪山。その中でもロープウェイとリフトで7合目まで上がることができる黒岳は大雪山登山の玄関口として賑わう。ほとんど初めてに近いハイクだった俺たちは、もともと体育会系育ちだったのが裏目に出た。まるで階段トレーニングで競争するかのようなペースでスタートしてしまったのだ。

「ぷはーっ！疲れたぁー！」

まだ 10分しか登っていないっていうのに、俺もイシカワもゆでタコのように顔を赤らめ、全身からムンムンと湯気を発している。

「いやぁ、登山ってハードだな。やたら喉が渇くよ」

グビグビビと音を立てて水を飲むイシカワ。俺もイシカワも、あっという間に半分を飲み干してしまった。ヤバい。このペースじゃ、すぐに水が底尽きてしまう。飲む量をセーブしていかなければ…。しかし、学習能力に乏しい俺たちは、相変わらずのハイペースで登っていった。サウナから上がってきたきた時みたいな、顎から滴るほどの汗。

「ダメだぁ。また喉渇いた〜！」

イシカワはザックをおろし、水筒をまさぐっている。

「あれ？ …あれれ？」とイシカワ。

「どした？」

「ザックの外にぶら下げていた水筒が…なくなってる」

無言でしばらく見つめ合う俺とイシカワ。

「なにやってんのよ！」

それからは、俺の水筒のわずかな水を2人でちびちび飲みながら山頂を目指した。

── ヤクルト飲んでるんじゃないんだから！

少ない水を見るたびに、水筒を落としたイシカワを呪った。こうして、なんとか黒岳の山頂に到着した。

「やったぁあああ！」

と二人で大きくバンザイしたのも束の間、次の瞬間には黒岳のさらに奥に佇む大斜面に釘づけになっていた。

「すっげぇ…」

北海道第二の高峰、北鎮岳である。豊富な残雪を湛えた北鎮岳の大斜面がキラキラと輝きを放ち、スキーヤーの到来を待っている…ように俺には見えた。

「イシカワ！ あれ滑ろうぜ！」

命の水はすでに底を突いており、時刻は既に15時。ロープウェイの最終便が18時だということも忘れている…というか、それ以前に全然時計を見てないのだ。北鎮岳方向に歩き始めると空気が変わった気がした。

黒岳山頂まで周りにいた春スキー愛好家の姿はなくなり、本格的山屋スタイルのおじさんとすれ違った。口は開かなくとも、表情が「山をなめるなよ」と言っている。しかし、北鎮岳の大斜面を睨みつけながら鼻息荒く突進していく俺たちは、そんなのお構いなしだった。そして、17時。北鎮岳山頂に到達。

「バ、バンザーイ！」

大学で眠そうに講義を聴いているか、飲み屋で酔っ払ってるかの付き合いだった俺とイシカワにとって、最高の達成感だった。その時、凄まじい北風が俺たちに容赦なく吹きつけてきた。とんでもない量の汗をかき、バケツの水を頭から被ったんじゃないかっていうくらい全身びしょ濡れだった俺とイシカワ。その汗が一瞬にして凍り付いていくようだった。

「さ、寒ううういいい！！」

"Oh, after all Daisetsuzan is wide."
While being blown by the wind at the top of the mountain, we three felt the benefits of climbing to the fullest.
A 360-degree panorama spread from the summit of Kurodake, and my eyes were pinned to the large slopes of Mt. Hokuchin and Mt. Kamikawa, which had a lot of snow. There is no skier who doesn't get excited when they see the slope of Mt. Kamikawa. A large, non-stressed slope that does not match the silhouette of the black and piercing ridgeline continues endlessly toward the bottom of the valley.
"Well, let's have fun!" I told the two cameramen and started running with my spring light equipment toward the summit of Mt. Kamikawa. I entered the valley from Mt. Keigetsu and Mt. Ryoun, gradually increasing the altitude while climbing along the mountainside. The crampons work super well on corn snows, and in the blink of an eye, I was approaching the peak of Mt. Kamikawa.

Key and Morishi were planning to aim at me from the opposite side of the valley, at the summit of Mt. Keigetsu. When I reached the peak, I waited for Key's radio for a while. Then I couldn't wait any more and starting to talk.
"Key, where are you now?"
"We are about the reach the top of the mountain… are you already at the top?"
"It's easier to climb than I expected."
"It's way too fast! Sorry we cannot find a place with a good view. Please wait a little longer."
After the radio communication, I looked back on the season with splendid view of the mountains. I had trained well during the "stay home" (state of emergency announced) period, then I had trained and prepared my body and mind in nature with trail running, MTB, SUP, etc. Before the season, I had been able to face myself and prepare well for my skiing as a "wild animal" with the necessary exercise, food, and rest. When had I had a season with such a good balance of mind and body? There had been a season when I was young that I was in similar physical condition to what I was in now, but it was the first time that I was so prepared mentally. Being in the wilderness well prepared—I'd always wanted this feeling.

The mountain next door is one kilometer away, so when Key and Morish were shooting me, I didn't feel their presence. I felt bad for both of them, but I decided to immerse myself in my enjoyment. I knew that such consciousness often resulted in good performance.

The first turn, I checked the feel of the corn snow, which had loosened moderately. I gained speed and took one more to reconfirm the condition.
"Got it!"
After that, I shifted to top gear and skied not with my head and logic but with my instincts and my heart. I let myself turn into a graceful wild animal, like an eagle flying in the sky, like a dolphin swimming in the ocean.
It was only a few tens of seconds filled with the spirit of adventure. This is the best way that I know to feel alive. When I reached the bottom, I was just laughing, looking up at the vast slopes. What was I worried about, and what was I hesitating for? Frightened by the invisible, confused by the rapidly changing human society…
Some may say that you have to adapt to change, but I think we should look more at the essence, something which never changes.
The snow that I was standing on, the wind stroking my cheeks, all the nature surrounding me are owned by nobody, I was immersed in the joy of being surrounded by priceless things. I tried to curve the splendid spurs of the magnificent mountains, but it's a tiny difference. On the earth, small ants and human beings are not so different.

Tシャツがベッタリと体に張り付き、容赦なく体温を奪ってくる。せめて温かいうちにTシャツの汗を搾っておくんだった…。あんなに楽しみにしていた滑降が一気に面倒に感じてきた。歯がカタカタと音を立てている。6月中旬だっていうのに、なんなんだこの寒さは！ こんなんだったら大人しくビーチで水着のギャルでも眺めてるんだった。結局、寒すぎて滑った記憶はほとんどゼロ。さらに最終のロープウェイにもキッチリ乗り遅れ、喉の渇きに喘ぎながら、雪解けの急峻な登山道をドロドロになりながらスキーを担いで下山。
途中で日没になり、獣の気配に怯え、歌を歌いながら歩いた。それにしても、熊に怯えながら歌う歌は、なんで必ず「森のくまさん」なんだ？

ほろ苦く、懐かしい思い出。もしかしたら、何も知らなかったあの頃が一番幸せな時だったのかもしれない。その後、間一髪で死ななかった体験が何度あっただろうか。そして、何人もの友人・知人を山で失ってきた。若い頃は、まるでドラゴンボールの孫悟空のように、天真爛漫に最強のスキーヤーを目指した俺も、山の怖さを知り、結婚して家族を養うようになると、さらに慎重になっていった。昔を懐かしみながら、春のザラついた斜面にクランポンを食い込ませていく。カランカランという金属音と、サクッサクッと粗目雪に食い込む音の小気味よい二重奏が風のない山に反響している。登りに没頭できるちょうどよい斜度を楽しみながら後ろを振り向くと、重い荷物

を背負った二人のカメラマンは、ほとんど足が止まっていた。
「腰いて〜」
基本的に、圭くんが快適そうに登っていることはまずない。腰が痛かったり、肩が痛かったり、体力的にしんどかったり、暑さにやられたりしても装備に関して妥協することはないのだ。俺たちが「滑りたい！」という溢れる欲求があるように、圭くんの「撮りたい！」という欲求は尋常ではないのだ。今日同行してくれた映像カメラマンのモリシ（森島和宏）にしてもそうだ。仕事になるかも分からない撮影のために、深夜出発で長距離ドライブし、重い三脚を含むデカザックを背負って、一人のスキーヤーを追いかけてくれるのだ。俺は本当に恵まれている。そう思っていた。

「おお〜、やっぱり大雪山は広いな〜」
3人は山頂の風に吹かれながら、登り切った恩恵を身体いっぱいに感じていた。黒岳の山頂から360度のパノラマが広がり、ひときわ残雪の多い北鎮岳と上川岳の大斜面に目が釘付けになった。上川岳の斜面を目にしたとき、テンションの上がらないスキーヤーはいないはずだ。黒く刺々しい稜線のシルエットとは似合わないノンストレスの大斜面が谷底に向かって延々と続いているのだ。
「そんじゃ、よろしく！」
俺は、2人のカメラマンにそう告げると、春装備の軽さを良いことに

上川岳山頂に向かって走って行った。桂月岳と凌雲岳のコルから谷に入り、山の腹を巻きながら徐々に高度を上げていく。クランポンがザラメ雪に面白い様に効き、あっと言う間に上川岳のピークが近づいてきた。圭くんとモリシは、桂月岳の山頂から狙う予定だった。山頂に着いて、しばらく圭くんたちの連絡を待っていたが、なかなか無線が入らないので、痺れを切らせて無線を入れた。
「圭くん、今どの辺ですか〜？」
「もうすぐ山頂だけど…もしかしてもう着いているの？」
「思ったより登りやすくて」
「早いね〜！ こっちは見渡しが良い場所が見当たらなくて。もう少し待っててね！」
無線交信を終えると、俺は山の景色を眺めながら今シーズンを振り返っていた。ステイホーム時期にトレーニングを積み上げ、そのあとはトレランやMTB、SUPなどで自然の中で身体と心を鍛え、整えていった。スキーを滑る野生動物として、必要な運動と必要な食事、必要な休息を心がけながら、スキーと真正面から向かい合えたシーズン前だった。こんなにも心身共にバランス良い状態で雪山にいるシーズンはいつぶりだろうか？ いや、若い頃も今によく似た身体の状態はあったけれど、ここまで心も整ったのは初めてだった。こうして、無駄のない存在として自然の中にいる喜び。この感覚をずっと求めていたのだ。

Well, when will the ski season end?
I don't always know. When I'm chasing the snow, my heart is so fulfilled that I can't decide when to end it. The snow that covered the land of Hokkaido gradually melts, and at the same time as the slopes turn black, the mountains accepting skiers quietly close their doors. In the midwinter, I had been able to move from peak to peak like a bird, but now I was struggling in the twenty-meter creeping pine belt. I know the more I extend my season, the more I lose my freedom in the mountains. However, I wanted to see the story through to its end, until the snow began to pile up and finally disappeared. Just as I had witnessed this winter's birth, this time I would witness winter passing away.

隣の山と言っても1kmも離れているので、遠すぎて撮影されている実感がなかった。二人には悪いけれど、自分のために滑ることに没頭させてもらおう。まぁ、そのような意識が結果的に良い作品に結びつくことが多いのを俺は知っていた。程よく緩んだコーンスノーの感触を確かめながら、まずは1ターン。もう少しスピードを上げ、再確認の1ターン。
「よし！」
あとは感じとったことを頭ではなく感覚で、思考ではなく感性によって、滑走という表現に変えていく。大空を飛ぶ鷲のように、大海原を泳ぐイルカのように、優美な野生動物であること。山に似合ったターンを刻むこと。大いなるロマンをターンに乗せていく。滑っているのは、ほんの数十秒。この数十秒以上に、自分が「生きている」と実感する術を俺は知らない。俺は谷底から広大な斜面を見上げながら、ただただ笑っていた。

何を心配し、何を迷っていたのだろうか？ 目に見えないものに怯え、目まぐるしく変化して見える人間社会に惑わされ…。変化に対応しなければならないと言われるけれど、もっと本質に目を向けるべきだと思うのだ。踏みしめている雪も、頬を撫でる風も、見渡す限りの大自然も誰のものでもない。俺は、値段を付けられないものに囲まれている喜びに浸っていた。雄大な山々に立派なシュプールをつけようっ

たって、この通りだ。この地球上において、小さなアリンコも人間も、さほど変わらない存在なのだ。
さて、スキーシーズンをいつ終えるのか。いつも分からない俺がいる。雪を追いかけている時の心があまりにも充実していて、その時期を終えるタイミングを自分でなかなか決めることができないのだ。北海道の大地をすっぽりと包んでいた雪も徐々に解けていき、斜面が黒くなっていくと同時に、スキーヤーに開かれた山は静かに扉を閉じていく。厳冬期は山のピークからピークへ鳥のように移動できていたのに、今はたった20mのハイマツ帯に行く手を阻まれ、悪戦苦闘している。粘れば粘るほどに、どんどん自由を失っていく現実を痛感するのは分かっている。
しかし、雪が積み始めて、最後に消えてなくなっていくまでの物語が完結するまで見届けたい自分がいた。
今シーズンという冬の出産に立ち会ったように、今度は冬の最期を看取るのだ。

雪解け 大雪高原沼

「今日は暑くなりそうだよね〜。きっと今日も上富良野と東川が最高気温を競うんだろうな」
圭くんが愉快そうに言った。この冬、特に馴染み深かった上富良野と東川。厳しい冬の寒さが印象的な街だけど、実は北海道の中でもトップレベル(?)に夏場は暑い街でもあるのだ。そろそろビーチに水着のギャルが出没する時期だけど、俺たちは性懲りもなくスキーを背負っていた。高速道路を疾走する車は上川層雲峡で下道に降りると、断崖迫る層雲峡を過ぎて大雪山の東側に回り込んでいく。やがて、豊富な雪渓を抱いた谷と、ひときわ大きな雪壁が現れた。一部のスキーヤー・スノーボーダーにとって夏スキーの最終目的地となる銀泉台と大雪高原温泉だ。このエリアは6月中旬にならないと通じるゲートがオープンにならないので、いわば夏スキー限定のオアシスなのだ。雪解けが進むと、雪の表面に雪解け水が流れた縦溝が刻まれ、さらにはスプーンカットというスプーンで雪面をえぐったような硬い凸凹で埋め尽くされる。これらの雪は、春のコーンスノーのように心地よい感触があるわけでもなく、スピードを出せるわけでもなく、ただただコントロールが極めて難しい雪なのだ。ここから先のシーズンは、長距離ドライブとロングハイク、夏並みの暑さといった負の要素と、滑ることで得られる満足感とを天秤にかけて、いつまで滑るのかを

決める感じだ。
どんなに物好きな滑り手でも、大体はスプーンカットになったら終了、というのがパターンだった。しかし、最近は新たな遊びが(変態の中で)一般化して、シーズンが少し伸びてきた。雪解け水が溜まった沼を滑るウォーターライドである。
今回の目的は、なかなか撮影できなかった新緑の中を滑走すること、そして、残雪期の代名詞であるスプーンカットを滑ること。ガタボコ雪に疲れたら、そのまま面ツルの沼に滑り込めば良い!
「銀泉台の方が登り始めから雪があるからいいんだけどな〜」
助手席でブツブツ言っているのは、スノードルフィン直系の後輩、小路口稔(ミノル)だ。ブツブツ言っているのはいつものことなので、先輩の独断と偏見で大雪高原温泉に車を走らせた。思えばミノルとも長い付き合いになった。俺がスノードルフィンの新米だった時、担当していた子供のレッスンをストーカーしていた高校生がミノルだった。当時のミノルは極度の人見知りだったけど、スキー好きには違いなかった。やがて、スノードルフィン主催の大会を手伝ってもらったり、一緒に滑ったりするようになり、彼が大学生になった時、半ば強引にスノードルフィンに引き込んだ。そこから、俺や佐々木大輔のようなハチャメチャな男の直属の後輩ということで、苦労も多かったと

思うけれど、今となっては、最も気を使わない友達なのだ。大雪高原温泉に到着すると、早速、ヒグマ情報センターに寄って熊の生息地での注意点などレクチュアを受けた。モニターに映し出されたのは、俺たちが滑ろうと思っている斜面を3〜4歳のガッチリした熊がよじ登っている映像だった。聞けば、これは昨日の映像だと言う。だからと言って大騒ぎすることではない。もともとこのエリアには熊が生息しており、毎日と言っていいほど目撃情報があるのだ。最近、札幌の東区で熊が人に危害を加える事故があった。山や海に隣接していない区に熊が出没したのは、実に驚きだった。人に危害を加えた熊は殺処分になってしまうのだが、そのニュースに対するネット上でのコメントを見て、俺は言いようのない違和感を感じていた。「人間のテリトリーに出てきたのだから殺処分は仕方ない…」これは人間サイドの考えだけれど、もっとよく考えてみたい。熊は山にいるという概念がそもそも間違っていて、もともと熊は北海道のどこにでもいた。熊にとっても生息しやすかった平野部を人間が奪ったことにより、熊が山に追いやられただけの話なのだ。アイヌの人たちにとって熊は神様だった。我々は、もっと自然の中で謙虚である必要はないだろうか。その点、スキーという自然にインパクトの少ない遊び道具で山にお邪魔する行為が、俺はとても気に入っているのだ。

Snowmelt Daisetsukougennuma

"It's going to be hot today. I'm sure Kami-Furano and Higashikawa will compete for the highest temperature today," Key said happily.
Kami-Furano and Higashikawa, two places that I was particularly familiar with this winter.
It's a city where the harsh winter cold is famous, but it is actually the hottest place in Hokkaido in summer.
It was about time for swimsuit girls to appear on the beach, but we were still skiing and snowboarding in the mountains. Getting off the highway at Kamikawa-Sounkyo, we passed through Sounkyo, a gorge, and approached the east side of Daisetsuzan. An abundant valley with a particularly large snow wall appeared. Ginsendai and Daisetsu Kogen Onsen are the final destinations for summer skiing for some skiers and snowboarders. This area is an oasis limited to summer skiing, as the gates leading to it will not open until mid-June. As the snow melts, a vertical gutter is carved on the surface of the snow; then the surface of the snow is filled with hard roughness that look like the snow surface has been scooped out with a spoon, called a spoon cut. These snows don't feel as comfortable as spring corn snow; they don't speed up; they're just extremely difficult to control. In the coming days, we would weigh the negative factors such as long-distance driving, long hikes, and summer heat against the satisfaction of skiing to decide how far we would ski. Normally, no matter how

enthusiastic the skier was, it would end when the snow surface was dominated by the spoon cut. But lately, with the introduction of a new item to enjoy the occasion (for some freaks), the season has lasted a bit longer. It is a water ski ride in a swamp filled with thawed water.
The purpose this time was to ski in the fresh green, which was difficult to shoot. And to slide the spoon cut, which is synonymous with the remaining snow season. If I got tired of rattling snow, I would just ski into the swamp with its smooth surface!

"I hope Ginsendai has snow from the beginning," Minoru Shoujiguchi, a junior who was directly affiliated with me at Snow-Dolphins, was murmuring in the passenger seat.
He always talks in small voice in the passenger seat, so I just drove to Daisetsu Kogen Onsen at my discretion and executed my opinion as the senior.
When I think about it, I have had a long history with Minoru. When I was newly hired at Dolphins, Minoru was a high school student who was stalking a child's lesson which I was in charge of. After that, he was forcibly drawn into Dolphins, and I think he had a lot of trouble because he was a junior who reported to a messy man like me, but now he is the least careful friend. Upon arriving at Daisetsu Kogen Onsen, we immediately stopped by the Brown

Bear Information Center and received a lecture on what to look out for in the bear habitat. What was projected on the monitor was a video of a three- to four-year-old bear climbing up the slope we were thinking of skiing on. We were informed that this was yesterday's video. That didn't mean we made a fuss. Bears lived in this area first, and there are almost daily sightings. Recently, there was an accident in Higashi-ku, Sapporo where a bear harmed people. This bear was slaughtered, but when I saw the comments on the internet about the news, I felt an indescribable discomfort.
"Since it appeared in the human territory, it can't be helped to slaughter it…"
This is a human-centric idea, but I want to think more about it. The concept that bears are in the mountains was wrong in the first place, as bears were originally everywhere in Hokkaido. It's just that bears were driven to the mountains by humans robbing the plains, which were easy for bears to live in. Bears were believed to be gods by the Ainu people. I think we need to be humbler in nature. In that respect, I really like how I visit the mountains by skiing, a way that has little impact on nature.
As I walked alternately on the mountain trail and on the snow, as I crossed several swamps where mizubashou (white skunk cabbage) flowers bloomed, the amount of snow remaining gradually increased, and the snow wall on the eastern side of Takanegahara was approaching.
Even though it was still on snow, the birch couldn't wait to spread its fresh

登山道と雪上を交互に歩きながら、水芭蕉の花が咲く沢をいくつか越えていくと、次第に残雪が多くなり、高根ヶ原東面の雪壁が近づいてきた。雪上だというのに、白樺も待ちきれずに新緑の葉を広げている。青空と新緑と残雪のコントラスト。そこに時折現れるグレイシャーブルーに光る沼。自然が織りなす妙に俺たちは言葉もなく、ただ感じ取ることだけでいっぱいいっぱいだった。ウォーターライドの沼（オアシス）には、意外にもたくさんの先客がいた。まぁ、たくさんの人と言っても、全員知っているあたりが呆れるばかりだけど、夏ならではのお楽しみをシェアする雰囲気は平和そのものだ。
オアシスはちょっと混雑していたので、俺たちは雪壁をハイクして1本滑ることにした。遠目には綺麗だった雪面も、近くで見ると無数の縦筋と落石で荒れていた。俺もミノルも縦溝に翻弄され、落石に少し怯え、「うううおおお！」と叫びながら滑り切った。大抵は1本滑ったらすぐにオカワリしたくなる欲張りな俺だけど、今、滑走量とは関係しない変な満足感がドッと押し寄せてきた。
「今シーズン滑り切ったど〜！」
滑り納めのタイミングは意識しなくても降ってくるのだ。その足でオアシスに向かうと、スノーボーダーの山ちゃん（山内一志）とツトム（中田奨）が遊び終えるところだった。彼らは、自分が心地よい場所に身を置くことを何よりも大切にしていた。二人と話していると、なぜか全てが平和に感じて、心がポカポカするのだ。そんな悟りの境地にいる山ちゃんが「タケさんに会えてよかった〜」と言ってくれたのが嬉しかった。

グレイシャーブルーに輝く高原沼に向け、真っ直ぐにスピードを上げていく。キンキンに冷えた氷水をたたえた沼が物凄い勢いで迫ってくるが、スピードを緩めずに思いっきり滑り込んでいく。着水した瞬間、まずスキーの滑りの良さに驚き、水面の滑らかさに驚く。水の感触を両スキーで楽しみながら、水面を撫でるようにターンを切っていく。ほとばしるスプレーというかスプラッシュ！ ほんの一瞬のことで、感触に浸るほどの時間はないけれど、雪も水もほとんど同じなのだ。あり得ないことだけど、水でできたビッグマウンテンを滑ったら気持ち良いんだろうな〜。そんな妄想に浸りながら、何度も登って滑ってを繰り返した。深まわりするほどにブーツは水没し、中は氷水でタプタプに満たされている。そうこうしているうちに寒さも限界に近づいてきたので、最後にミノルと同時に滑り込み、同時にスプレーをあげるセッションで〆にすることにした。しかしミノル、こういう時に限ってやらかす癖は、高校生の時から全く変わっていない。バランスを崩して半身ダイブ！ ドボンと勢いよく立ち上がった水柱に俺は激突して、頭からずぶ濡れになってしまった。
「うおい！ ミノルー！！」
笑い声が山間に響き渡った。

green leaves.
The contrast between the blue sky, fresh green, and the remaining snow. The glacier blue glowing swamp that occasionally appeared in the remaining snow. We were just enjoying the beauty of nature wordlessly.
Surprisingly, the Water Ride swamp had many predecessors.
Well, even if you say a lot of people, I'm just surprised that we all know each other, but the atmosphere of sharing the fun unique to summer skiing is peaceful. The oasis was a bit crowded, so we decided to hike the snow wall and enjoy the skiing there.
The snow surface, which was beautiful from a distance, was rough with countless vertical stripes and falling rocks when viewed up close. Both Minoru and I were tossed by the vertical flutes, and we both were a little scared of the falling rocks and screamed down the slope. Most of the time, I'm a greedy person who wants to keep skiing as soon as I ski once, but now I was suddenly feeling a strange sense of satisfaction that had nothing to do with the amount of skiing.
"I've skied through this season!"
The end of the season had just been announced without my awareness.

I sped up straight toward the glacier blue shining plateau swamp. The swamp filled with ice water approached with tremendous speed, but I glided as hard as possible without slowing down. The moment I landed on the water, I was first surprised by the smoothness of the movement of my skis and the smoothness of the water surface. While enjoying the feel of the water on both skis, I made turns as if smoothly touching the surface of the water. It was just a moment—I didn't have enough time to immerse myself in this, but snow and water are almost the same.
I know it is impossible, but it would be nice to ski on a big mountain made of water. While immersed in such a phantasm, I climbed and skied many times. The deeper I turned, the more my boots got submerged and filled with ice-cold water. As I continued, the cold approached the limit. So, we, Minoru and I, decided to finish today with session of skiing in at the same time and making a spray at the same time. However, Minoru is Minoru. His habit of messing things up only at this kind of good moment hasn't changed at all since he was in high school.
He lost his balance and half his body dived into the swamp, making a big splash of water! I crashed into the water pillar he had made and got soaked from my head to my toes.
"What the hell! Minoru!!"
A big laugh echoed in the mountains.

擦り切れ、ドロドロになったスキーウェア。穴が空いたグローブ。
毛羽立ったスキーの滑走面。1シーズン滑り切ったスキー用具は、満身
創痍でありながら、満足気に微笑んでいるように見えた。道具たちと
同じように、俺たちも身体のあちこちが痛いけれど、ボロボロに日焼
けした満足面を下げて、雪のない登山道をゆっくりと下山していた。
「やりきったね…」
圭くんの穏やかな表情がすべてを物語っていた。
コロナ禍で海外への遠征をキャンセルしたとき、世界がギューッと
狭まってくる不安を覚えた。しかし、それは気持ちの問題だった。
冒険とか旅とか言ってみても、人生の一部分を切り取って言っている
だけで、人生自体が冒険であり、旅なのだ。
我々は、朝起きた時、自分次第で今までにない一日を始めることが
できる。
同じ散歩道でも、歩くスピードや視点を変えることで新たな発見が
できるし、あえて迷ってみたりすると、新しい発見の刺激だらけだ。
そこに自然のミステリアスな世界がプラスされ、四季による様々な
変化が加わる。
この北海道を旅し続けたとしても、好奇心が尽きることなどないのだ。
最近、マイクロツーリズムという観光のあり方が提案されている。
観光名所を順番に巡り、行った事実に満足する観光から、身近で
あっても、もっとクリエイティブで冒険的な観光が求められていくだろう。

そういう意味で北海道はとてつもないポテンシャルを持っている。
コロナが収束したら…やっぱり海外に旅に出ると思う。
しかし、以前のように出られないことに対する焦りはもうなかった。
北海道にいるだけでワクワクし、北海道にいるだけで安心感がある。
まだまだこれからも、ずっと遊ばせてもらうことにしよう。

rayed and muddy ski wear. A glove with a hole. A roughened ski gliding
surface. The ski equipment that skied through for whole season seemed to
be smiling with satisfaction, even though it was full of damages.
Like these materials, our bodies were hurt all over, but we were slowly
getting down the snow-free mountain trail with tanned face smiling with
satisfaction.
"We've done it…"
Key's gentle expression tells everything.
When we canceled the expedition abroad with the corona pandemic, I was
worried that the world would narrow tightly. But it was matter of how we
think about.
Adventure or travel is part of your life, just by cutting out a part of your life,
life itself is an adventure and a journey. We can start a brand new day on
your own when we wake up in the morning. Even on the same walking path,
you can make new discoveries by changing the walking speed and
viewpoint, and if you dare to get lost, you will face a lot of new discoveries.
The mysterious world of nature is added to it, and various changes are
added depending on the four seasons. Even if I continue to travel to
Hokkaido, my curiosity will never run out.
Recently, 'Micro-tourism' has been proposed during this difficult situation. I
think that people starting to get attracted by more creative and adventurous
sightseeing at some where more close by, than the tourism that you go
around the tourist attractions in order and are satisfied with the fact that you

went there. In that sense, Hokkaido has tremendous potential.
When this pandemic is over, I think I will go on a trip abroad. But I was no
longer impatient about not being able to travel abroad like I used to. Just
being in Hokkaido is super exciting for me, and also gives me a sense of
security. I will enjoy forever and continue to play.

Minoru Shojiguchi

Minoru Shojiguchi

And a new season will come around...

FIELD EARTH

星野リゾート トマム

KA**M**UI
SKI LINKS

Prince Grand Resort
Furano

Rider Tadahiro Yamaki

HIGASHIKAWA
THE TOWN OF
PHOTOGRAPHY

Takashi Kodama   Prince Grand Resort Furano

HPB

Hokkaido Powder Belt

Prince Grand Resort
Furano

SKI LINKS

Hoshino Resorts
TOMAMU